*Recovering from the
Loss of a Child*

Katherine Fair Donnelly

Recovering from the Loss of a Child

Macmillan Publishing Company, *New York*
Collier Macmillan Publishers, *London*

Macmillan Publishing Company
866 Third Avenue, New York, N.Y. 10022
Collier Macmillan Canada, Inc.

Library of Congress Cataloging in Publication Data
Donnelly, Katherine Fair.
    Recovering from the loss of a child.
    Bibliography: p.
    Includes index.
    1. Bereavement—Psychological aspects.
2. Children—Death.   3. Parent and child.
I. Title.
BF575.G7D66   1982   155.9'37   82-12785
ISBN 0-02-532150-1

10 9 8 7 6 5 4

Macmillan books are available at special discounts for bulk purchases for sales promotions, premiums, fund-raising, or educational use. Special editions or book excerpts can also be created to specification. For details, contact:

> *Special Sales Director*
> *Macmillan Publishing Company*
> *866 Third Avenue*
> *New York, New York, 10022*

Printed in the United States of America

Grateful acknowledgment is made to the following for permission to reprint previously published material:

Reproduced from *A Boy Thirteen: Reflections on Death,* by Jerry A. Irish. Copyright © 1975 The Westminster Press. Reproduced by permission.

For excerpts from SHARE, "Booklet on Starting a SHARE Group," SHARE, St. John's Hospital, 800 E. Carpenter, Springfield, Illinois 62702.

"Do's and Don'ts—Helping Bereaved Parents," Copyright © 1979 Lee Schmidt, Parent Bereavement Outreach, 535 16th Street, Santa Monica, California 90402. Reprinted with permission.

The Compassionate Friends, "Understanding Grief," Copyright © 1980, The Compassionate Friends, Inc., P.O. Box 1347, Oak Brook, Illinois 60521. Reproduced with permission. The Compassionate Friends, "Suggestions For Doctors and Nurses," Copyright © 1981 The Compassionate Friends. Reproduced with permission.

For excerpts from *Sudden Infant Death Syndrome: Its Impact on Parents, Neighbors and Friends—from a Father's Perspective,* by Leo C. Lefebvre, Jr. Revised April 1979. Published by the Council of Guilds for Infant Survival, Inc., Washington, D.C.

For excerpts from *Living with an Empty Chair: A Guide Through Grief,* by Dr. Roberta Temes, Downstate Medical Center. Copyright © 1977 by Mandala. Published by Irvington Publishers, Inc., New York.

For excerpts from *Collected Poems,* Harper & Row. Copyright 1917, 1945 by Edna St. Vincent Millay.

CONTENTS

viii · CONTENTS

Our society has perpetrated a fraud. We are led to believe that the last thing bereaved parents would want to do is talk about the death of their child. The complete reverse is true. Parents *want* to talk and *want* someone to listen. Someone who can hear the crying of their soul: "I am never going to hear the sound of my child's voice again. I will never see his face. I will never touch her hair. I will never see my child's smile again."

This book is not intended to be a statistical survey. Rather, it is concerned with the human element—those deep and raw emotions that pervade our daily lives. There isn't any way one can adequately express in writing what a parent feels at the death of a child—living through it, surviving it, putting one foot in front of the other, and getting past one more day.

No one can suffer for us. There is little that can be said to lessen the intensity of the pain, for one never fully recovers from the loss of a child. Yet there is a sense of comfort to be derived from those who have undergone such a nightmare. Families who have "been there" speak what is unspeakable—in the hope that other bereaved families will hear they are not alone in their agonizing despair. Listening to parents and siblings who have traveled that path offers a lifeline of support—a lifeline to survival.

To convey that spirit of survival, courageous parents and young people share with us their thoughts and inner feelings about such devastating grief and its effect on them. They tell the ways they found of coping—how they began to go to a movie again, how they began to tell a joke again, how they began to have sex again, how they began to face holidays again, how they began to live again. The awareness that other families have found strength to endure life's harshest hurt enables the bereaved to hear the message conveyed: "We know. We understand. We have been through it. You are not alone!"

One parent sums it up: "As we recover from a serious accident or surgery, so we recover from the emotional traumas in life; the sharp pain fades to a dull ache; the wound heals, but the scars remain forever. We learn to live with the memories, the lost hopes and shattered dreams. We never 'get over' the death, but we do 'recover,' adjust and learn to live with our pain."

The real-life experiences of the caring parents and surviving children, who bravely came forward to reach out in an effort to offer comfort and hope, should be a source of reassurance and help to all those who wish to survive.

It is also hoped that their experiences in living with the loss of a child will serve to enlighten all those seeking to provide consolation to bereaved families.

They tell it like it is—and it's tough!

ACKNOWLEDGMENTS

This book would not be complete without thanking:

Al and Trudy Zomper, two special people, for their loving ways and for being there when I need them.

The organizations involved in helping bereaved families:
The Compassionate Friends, Inc.; St. John's SHARE; SHARE Support Groups; The National Sudden Infant Death Syndrome Foundation; The Council of Guilds for Infant Survival; The Information and Counseling Programs for Sudden Infant Death; The National Tay-Sachs & Allied Diseases Association; AMEND; Unite; Hoping; Care; Hopes; Bereaved Parents; Wee Care; AIID; Pend; Sharing Heart; Kinder-Mourn; T.L.C.; Cure; Hand; Caretakers; Parents of Murdered Children; Candlelighters; The Candlelighters Foundation; The Centers for Attitudinal Research; Parent Bereavement Outreach; The Gold Star Mothers; The American Association for Marriage and Family Therapy; National Mental Health Association.

Jane Cullen, who always responded with compassion and warm enthusiasm for this undertaking and whose fine editorial touch added immeasurably to the final manuscript.

John H. Donnelly, Jr., whose guiding hand and heart were given many times into the wee hours in listening to and reading this manuscript, and without whose encouragement and support this work could not have been accomplished.

Angela and Peter Purpura, who gave so generously of their time in many ways: helping contact parents and siblings who shared their experiences; offering suggestions for the content of the book; listening to materials in various stages and reading still other portions for clarity in conveying the thoughts of bereaved families. They cannot be commended highly enough for the splendid effort they put forth in making this book one of help and hope.

Patricia Orlando Savi, who gave tirelessly of her time and energies. She was there at all times—as she always is.

Abraham Malawski, a special human being, whose wisdom, perception, and gentle caring added so much and helped in very many ways.

Betty J. Kelly, who diligently helped with research and painstakingly read the manuscript in its many stages.

Glenn Cowley, a support network par excellence and a superb agent.

Ruth Hannon, whose encouragement and help bolstered us from the onset.

Ann Lisa Magid, who listened with enthusiasm and helped ad infinitum.

Rose Fair, the Arkinds, Fairs, and Zompers for their steadfast faith and support.

The many individuals kind enough to hear or read this manuscript in its various stages, permitting me their thoughts and comments, and who helped in many other ways:

Marian Balster, Rev. Donald Balster, Chris Blenninger, Paulette Copia, Amy Farrugia, Lauren Gelband, Vivian Kessler, Sister Jane Marie Lamb, Leo C. Lefebvre, Jr., Marjorie Martin, Ruth Neubauer, Barbara Okst, Arthur F. Peterson, Jr., Ronnie Peterson, Dr. Berthold Schwarz, Harold Sherman, Eloise Shields, John L. Travis, and Lydia Volpe.

Jane Herman, whose copy editing and checking of last-minute details added considerably to the appearance and content of this book.

Steve Malawski, for his patience and understanding in listening, and for being the special brother and son that he is.

And a MOST SPECIAL THANK YOU to Miss Cara Purpura for the insight of her wise eight years.

Part One

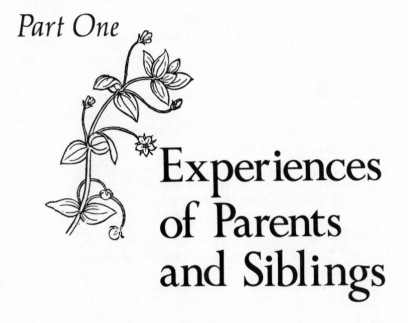

Experiences of Parents and Siblings

Getting on with living doesn't mean parents have to feel disloyal to their child's memory. Recovering doesn't mean you have to forget. You will always remember. So why not remember the good things in your child's life.

—Dr. and Mrs. Allen Haimes, bereaved parents

1 · A Child Dies

"It's six o'clock. If only I can make it until seven o'clock. Please, God, just help me make it to seven. I feel so numb. Yet I have this searing pain in my head. I know I am awake. There is this piercing hurt in my heart. I thought surely when I woke up this morning, I would tell myself what a terrible nightmare I'd had. And then I would be able to shake my head and say, 'This isn't real. My son is not dead.' But it wasn't a dream. Dear God, it wasn't a dream. If only I can make it until seven o'clock."

Judith Haimes, whose sixteen-year-old son, Michael, was killed in an automobile crash, was describing her initial responses to the loss of her son: the deep depression, the tightening feelings of the throat, the somatic distress lasting from ten minutes to hours at a time, the choking feeling with shortness of breath. Would she ever be able to make it to eight o'clock once she had gotten to seven?

The nightmare began on December 19, 1980. At four o'clock that afternoon Judith was preparing dinner. Her son Michael was getting ready to go to work. First, he had to drop some books off at the library. Michael kissed his mother goodbye and went out the door—never to return. At about the time Michael left the house, his father, Allen Haimes, left his dental practice early in order to pick up a younger son, Joshua, who had been visiting nearby with his grandmother. While Allen and Joshua were en route home, an ambulance raced by, its sirens blasting. Joshua turned to his father and made mention of it. Allen nodded. "Yes, Joshua, someone is hurt, and the ambulance is taking him to the hospital, where the doctors will make him better." Little did they know it was their Michael who was being rushed for help in the speeding ambulance.

A short time after Allen and Joshua arrived home, there was a knock at the door. It was a policeman who said that there had been an accident and Michael had been involved. The officer knew Michael and had wanted to come personally to tell the parents. He said the last time he had talked to their son, Michael had been bragging about what a great dad he had. "And I just felt it wouldn't be right for you folks to get a phone call about this."

Judith asked the officer if her son was all right. He replied, "Well, ma'am, he was still alive when I left him, at least for the moment." Judith felt a sensation that she had never felt before. She felt everything leaving from the top of her head to the bottom of her feet, almost a trancelike state. She sensed her son was already dead. A mother's instinct told her so. But the officer assured her that he had been there when the ambulance arrived and Michael was taken out of the car—still alive. The policeman suggested they get their car and follow him to the hospital.

As they drove behind the officer, Judith told Allen to be prepared that when they got to the hospital Michael would be dead. Allen asked her how she knew this. "Because my heart stopped a few minutes ago," Judith replied. At this point there were no tears, just shock and numbness. Allen tried to reassure his wife. "You're just upset. Everything is going to be all right."

They parked at the hospital's emergency entrance. As Judith got out of the car, she urged Allen to listen to her. "Please understand that Michael is dead. I know he is dead."

Allen became a little annoyed and replied, "He is *not* dead. I'm sure he's not dead. God wouldn't let that happen to us."

When they entered the hospital, a nurse sat them down quietly and told them the medics were working on their son. Judith asked, "How can they still be working on him?" The nurse advised them that Michael was still alive.

As Judith and Allen sat in a quiet room, pandemonium

broke out nearby. They heard the loudspeaker urgently paging the thoracic surgeon, then paging the neurosurgeon, everybody shouting orders, everyone deeply involved with Michael. Allen was holding Judith, repeating over and over that everything would be all right. "Nothing is going to happen to Michael, not to our Michael," he assured her. After what seemed like an eternity, Judith began thinking like a human being again, the way a mother would think. She heard the doctors and nurses talking, ordering blood, and she thought: My God, maybe they can save him. Maybe they can bring him back. Maybe I was wrong. Maybe what I felt wasn't my heart stopping. Maybe he really is alive and is just very seriously hurt and, oh, everything is going to be all right.

The door kept opening. People were coming in and out. Judith suddenly realized when more people entered the room that perhaps one of them was going to tell her Michael was dead. And she didn't want to know that. She asked no one be allowed in except the staff physicians, Dr. Borota or Dr. Heller, both of whom were friends of the Haimeses. Judith didn't want to see strange faces, and she certainly didn't want a strange face to tell her that her son was dead. After a while Dr. Borota walked into the room. Judith looked at him—a very strong man, a man who faces death a dozen times a week, being a specialist in head and neck cancer. Dr. Borota was also the godfather of the Haimeses' youngest child, Ian. "When Dr. Borota came in, he didn't say anything. Then he began to cry. And when he cried, we knew." Michael Steven Haimes, aged sixteen, was dead.

"On the first anniversary of Cassandra's death the realization that it had been one full year since I had seen my child was utterly devastating." Angela Purpura was describing the anguish she and her husband, Peter, felt during the difficult period one year after their eight-year-old daughter had died of an inoperable brain stem tumor.

Angela's thoughts went back to a bright, sunny day in May,

when her two daughters were making what they called Purple Cows, an unholy combination of milk and grape juice. It sounded like a ghastly concoction, but the girls loved it. However, Cassandra vomited. That was the beginning of Cassandra's illness. It was her primary symptom. It was also the beginning of a time of great frustration for Angela and Peter. The doctors could find nothing wrong with their daughter and dismissed it as a virus—a virus that never went away because Cassandra never stopped vomiting. Later the doctors attributed her problem to a urinary tract infection. But a test proved negative. Any parent who has lost a child to a terminal illness will readily understand the anxieties and feelings of helplessness Angela and Peter Purpura experienced at this time. The doctors kept coming up with blanks. However, Angela *knew* her child was sick. She sensed that Cassandra was terribly ill. Nothing the pediatricians told her could alter her opinion. The doctors asked Angela what she thought was wrong with Cassandra. Angela replied she was fearful of leukemia. The doctors assured her the blood tests were negative. Nonetheless, Angela insisted that her daughter be hospitalized because of dehydration. Against their wishes, the doctors did so. However, they found nothing wrong with Cassandra, and she was again returned home. Angela was beside herself. "You can't just send her home this way. She is going to continue vomiting. You have to do something for her."

In desperation, Angela took Cassandra to a physician near her home. The doctor saw a problem in Cassandra's eyes and discovered it was a neurological disorder. The child was taken to the emergency room of a local hospital, which Angela felt by far was the most positive hospital experience they had. "They were very caring, very responsive, and very kind." The neurologist recommended that a CAT scan be done. But it proved negative. Although a brain tumor was initially suspected, it was ruled out after the test had been run. Cassandra continued vomiting. At this point she was transferred to a larger hospital. It was more than a month before her illness was diagnosed. What was not visible on the initial CAT scan was *very* visible three weeks later. By that time the brain tumor was far advanced. When the Purpuras discovered this, they chose not to leave Cassandra in the hospital because the pediatric neurologists offered them no hope. Radiation to inhibit the growth of the tumor was suggested. But Angela and Peter felt that while it might give their daughter a couple of more months at the most, it was a big price to pay for what Cassandra would have to endure. Angela told the neurologists, "Cassandra cannot afford to vomit one more time." The doctors wanted Cassandra in the hospital on an inpatient basis for three to six weeks. But Cassandra did not have that much time left. Peter and Angela chose to keep their small daughter at home—in a comfortable, loving, caring environment no hospital could possibly have given her. Because they wanted to make sure that her last days were in a familiar surrounding, they turned their large family room into a hospice to care for their dying child.

In preparing her daughter for receiving last rites, Angela didn't know what to say to the child since theirs was not a religious family. It had been some time since Cassandra had last spoken. Angela had no way of knowing if her daughter could hear her, as she had learned that hearing tends to be the last sense to go. But Angela held her child's hand and softly said to her, "Cassandra, honey, Mommy just called St. Boniface, and a young priest is going to be coming here to the house, and he will be saying some prayers over you." Angela paused. She didn't know what else to say. There was no book she had ever read, but somehow she had to prepare her child for death. Suddenly Angela was taken aback. "I can't tell you the shock I experienced when Cassandra replied. She said to me, *very clearly,* 'When is he coming?' Now you have to understand she had a brain tumor and toward the end could not speak well. But her words 'When is he coming?' were spoken so clearly, I was astonished. So not only did she hear me, but she was able to respond to what I said. I comforted her and told her he would be here in a little while."

Cassandra Purpura was both baptized and given last rites on August 31, 1979. She died the next day—on her mother's thirty-eighth birthday.

Alan Hollender's father died when he was nine years old. Having idolized his dad, the boy became a lost soul. His grades began to fall. He became resentful, restless, and soon fell into the drug scene at his local school. His father's two brothers developed close relationships with the boy. But this was to be short-lived, too. Both uncles died at early ages of heart conditions, a congenital health problem in their family. Lost again at age fifteen, and looking for a male image in his life, Alan turned to his grandfather. But the boy again experienced the trauma and heartache of death. His grandfather died soon thereafter.

When Alan started being absent from school, his mother, Leonora, was summoned. He had gotten in with a bad crowd and was now deeply into drugs. Earlier his mother had found pot while cleaning his room. When Alan discovered this, he became furious and put a lock on his door. He began to berate his mother and threaten her. He wanted money from her. Leonora worked for a doctor nearby but did not have the amount of money Alan demanded of her. One morning Leonora received a telephone call telling her that her son had been apprehended in a theft at her employer's office. Unknown to Leonora, Alan had taken the keys from her bag and gone to rob the doctor's office. However, police saw the lights on and captured Alan during the burglary attempt. Leonora engaged an attorney. Alan was only seventeen. He was sent to Rikers Island for several days, as the attorney desired. In the hope that it would discourage any future thought of criminal activity, he wanted Alan to get a brief taste of what it was like to be imprisoned. Alan was put on probation. But he was still into drugs. His mother didn't know how to handle the problem and sought aid at a neighborhood agency where there was an encounter group. She tried to discuss the problem but was asked to bring her son. When she told the group Alan refused to come, she was advised to turn him in to the authorities. Leonora felt she could not do this.

"Alan grew up in the worst era of drugs in the schools. He was lonely, and from the day his father died, he appeared completely lost. No matter how I tried to reach him, he was never able to accept his father's death. Once when I came home, I found him spaced out in his room, so completely abnormal in his reactions I knew it was more than pot. At other times he fought with me on almost every issue. He didn't seem to really know what he wanted. No one seemed to be able to penetrate that shell of loneliness, even though he had a lot of friends." He wanted to get an apartment of his own. Leonora encouraged the move, and he found a small basement apartment nearby. But when the arrangements fell through, he became despondent. "He began to lie around in his room a great deal of the time and play his stereo." Now nineteen, tall, handsome, and with a couple of girl friends, Alan was also moody and often retreated to his bedroom to hear his music.

So, when Leonora returned home one Friday evening in 1974, after a game of canasta with friends, she did not consider it unusual to hear her son's stereo set playing. Not surprised, she undressed and went to bed around 11:30 P.M. At midnight the telephone rang. It was one of Alan's girl friends. Leonora remembers the phone call vividly. "She was very excited and was screaming. She said Alan had brought over his bankbook and some of his personal effects, and she thought he might have been thinking of suicide. The girl had already called the police, and they arrived just as I put the phone down. The door to Alan's room was locked, and the police broke it down. They found Alan sprawled over the bed. He had overdosed himself. I fell completely apart. The police called the ambulance because he was unconscious." Leonora saw them take her son into the ambulance but could not accompany them. She felt like jelly. Nothing would move. Her arms, her legs were immobile. A friend came to stay with her. The police called Leonora from the hospital and said they thought Alan was going to be all right, that they were pumping out his stomach. She couldn't believe this was happening. She began to drink scotch. Then the police called and told her she had better come to the hospital. When Leonora got there, her son was dead. A note was found later among his belongings, addressed to no one in particular, just a statement. A statement of a nineteen-year-old boy against the unknown face of death, now known to him only too well.

Danny Uhl, age sixteen, wasn't feeling well. He had a cold and was home that week, taking the usual cold medications. It was nothing startling. He returned to school right after the Christmas holidays. The first day back, he stayed late and went to basketball practice in the evening. Instead of coming home at 7:00 P.M., he came home at 9:00 P.M. He ate, took a shower, and went to bed. The next morning Danny awoke with chest pains. When she learned this, his mother, Ellen, immediately telephoned the doctor. As Danny headed back toward his bedroom, he screamed out, "My leg went dead." Ellen's other son, Michael, nineteen, began to massage his brother's leg in efforts to revive the circulation. Ellen called the doctor again, and an ambulance was summoned. Later the doctor advised Ellen that the diagnosis was a dissected aneurysm of the aorta, and a ten-hour operation was performed. During this time the doctors had to freeze the boy's body for twenty-five minutes. Fortunately no brain damage resulted. Danny was placed in an intensive care unit for five days. He seemed to be rallying, teasing the nurses that he wanted a beer—a beer he was never to have. Danny died on January 14, 1981, five days after surgery.

———

In the early afternoon of July 28, Norman Davis, age twenty, was brutally stabbed and died on the lawn in front of his parents' house. Young Norman, who was working for a swimming pool company, had finished early that day and decided to head home. Hours later his mother, Barbara Davis, was returning from the supermarket and found the street blocked. Police cars were everywhere. When they learned her identity, the police took Barbara to a neighbor's house and told her there had been a terrible tragedy. Barbara's first thought was that a friend of her son's, who had been helping him with some painting, had fallen off a scaffold. The police advised Barbara it was not her son's friend, but her own son, who had been killed. Stunned, Barbara asked if her son had been shot and was informed he had been stabbed. An hour later Sidney Davis learned the devastating news of his son's death. The details were too agonizing to comprehend.

Later the police determined that upon arriving home early, their son encountered two men who had just come from ransacking the house. By one pretext or another, the robbers got Norman back into the house, where they stabbed him several times. As they were outside leaving, they found they had forgotten the loot and went back inside. Norman, who was still alive, ran past his attackers down the steps and out of the house. The intruders gave chase and caught up with him on the front lawn, where they stabbed him again and fled. A short time later a neighbor heard the Davis family's dog barking outside and discovered Norman lying on the lawn. But it was too late. And although his attackers were ultimately caught—two drug addicts who were picked up on burglary charges in a nearby town—the fact remained: Norman Davis was dead. He was murdered in his own home by strangers—strangers who brought grief in a swift and merciless way to Barbara and Sidney Davis.

"You know, Mrs. Young, I had a dream about your little boy the other night. I saw him with some other kids who were trying to get him to come with them to sniff some glue. And your son told them, 'No, my mama will get mad.' And he kept telling them he didn't want any of that stuff." Doris Young was listening to a local merchant who had been concerned enough about this dream to speak of it to her. When Doris asked which son he had dreamed about, because she had three young boys, the shopkeeper replied, "The one who can never get the buttons closed on his coat." Doris knew immediately he was referring to her son Irvin, age eight. She thanked the storekeeper for telling her, and as she turned to leave, he cautioned her, "You watch out for him, Mrs. Young." For many days after this, Doris kept a close vigil over Irvin but, with other children and other duties, the shopkeeper's warning receded in her mind. Too, a mother does not wish to think of her child as being in a situation harmful to him, one where she cannot help.

One afternoon about a month later Doris was going to the grocery store. It was her practice when she left her house to take her children with her, and she did so on this occasion. That is, all except Irvin. He was outside playing with his favorite little girl friend, Penny. As Doris and her other children were leaving the house, she turned to Irvin and instructed him to come along with them. Irvin balked. He wanted to play with Penny. His mother was insistent. Reluctantly Irvin dragged behind them as Doris and the children continued en route to the store. At the corner Doris met two neighboring women, with several of their children. Together they crossed the street to the grocery store. Upon turning around, Doris saw Irvin was not with them. However, she wasn't worried. She thought he had returned to play with Penny. Nonetheless, she sent another son, Robby, age ten, to go get his brother and bring him back. But Penny was no longer playing in front of the house, and Irvin was nowhere to be found. When Robby returned to report this to his mother, the family returned home. Doris checked first at Penny's house, thinking surely her son had gone there. But he was not with Penny. Where then was her child? Doris and neighbors began to search everywhere, refrigerators, basements, but still there was no sign of the boy. Some hours later, after the search had proved futile, the police were called. Doris was distraught and kept phoning the police. "Being black and part of a minority, I felt they were not devoting time to finding out what happened to my child." The next afternoon at four o'clock her husband was notified the boy had been located. When told the news, Doris fainted; her son was found, drowned, lying between two rocks in the Hudson River.

2 · This Can't Be Real

...This isn't real.
   Signing the hospital release.
...This isn't happening.
   Calling the funeral home.
...It's a fantasy. I dreamed it.
   We have to get a casket.
...It's real ... she's dead ... she died.
   We have to get her clothes for the funeral.
...I want to scream, "No! No! No!"
   This can't be real.

And later:
   I want to be alone.
   NO! DON'T LEAVE ME ALONE!
   All the people, crying, mourning.
   And inside I am screaming,
   "Go home! NO, STAY!"

Parents experience excruciating pain and terrifying thoughts during the initial period of grief. One such parent, Angela Purpura, tells of the utter desolation after her daughter's death. "During the time of her illness, the emptiness was bearable because there was always a ray of hope, the slim chance some new miracle medicine would be discovered, or there would be a new breakthrough that would allow her recovery. When she died, the despair was overwhelming. I would look in her room, expecting to see her in the bed, yet knowing she would not be. I wanted to reach out to caress her, only to reach out to nothingness—sheer and total emptiness." Each time Angela enters church, she is reminded of the small white coffin and the funeral service that was celebrated in memory of their little girl. The tears come, and she wonders: Did it all really happen?

Another mother, who had just taken her two surviving children back to school for the first time since the funeral of her son, describes her anguish upon returning home. "I came into an empty house. My chest ached. There were no more wet tears, only the dry ones inside me that rammed against my chest. It was a racking pain. I went into the kitchen, sat down, and looked around the room. My mind kept seeing the children—*all* the children—here in happier times. I jumped up and pounded on the table. Why? Why? Why?" On the next school day she could no longer return directly to her house. She could not bear the terrible pain of being alone. She began to stop at the bakery shop, then at the hardware store, then at the dry cleaner's. Just to be in the presence of people, just to talk—about anything—until it was time to go pick up her children. Many months later this mother was able to utilize those hours in a foundling hospital. She found a way to relieve this great loss in her life by helping small infants who were alone and in pain. "There was no way I could bring back my son. But I felt that helping these small children was like a gift to my child."

After her son's suicide Leonora Hollender was driven home from the hospital by the police. A friend stayed with her. When she went to the closet, she saw her son's jacket and became hysterical, screaming, "I can't believe it." A day later detectives came to the house, as is customary after a suicide. This just can't be happening, Leonora kept thinking. She was beside herself. After the detectives left, she had to go to the bathroom. She could not because to do so meant she would have to pass her son's room. Instead, she used the facilities of a neighbor and continued this practice until she finally moved to a smaller apartment. At the funeral parlor Leonora was hysterical and was lying over the casket when suddenly a barrage of verbal accusations was hurled at her. Her son's girl friend, who had telephoned her about the possible suicide attempt, and the girl's mother began to scream at Leonora, "You killed him. You killed him." Help had to be summoned. "The police removed these people from the funeral parlor, but later they came to the funeral and started again. They telephoned me late at night. They called at my office. It was terrible. I later wondered why—if they thought my son was going to commit suicide—why, oh, why had they let him go home? At least they had some inkling of it. I didn't."

When her young son was found drowned, Doris Young's grief was inconsolable. She kept calling the police for weeks thereafter in an attempt to determine the true story of what had happened to her child. It was almost a form of hysteria, a compulsion to find the cause of her son's death. "I felt the police were not devoting the time necessary to finding out what happened to my child. I felt they were not investigating it thoroughly." The police came to see Doris one day. They told her that her son died as a result of an accidental drowning. The police theorized he might have gone with some boys to play on the rocks. And although some of the kids might have known what happened, they were afraid to speak. At the funeral the neighborhood parents came with their children to pay their respects. Doris noticed one young boy, a friend of her son's. The boy approached her with a wreath and cried hysterically. "That little boy was really very upset. He and Irvin were always together, and he was more than beside himself. The other children who came just kind of looked around and were uncomfortable. But this little boy cried and cried. I always felt that possibly he knew something more but would not or could not say."

Jane Birnbaum's husband was out of town when their son, Tony, was killed. Jane telephoned her husband in California, where he was working. She told him only there had been a bad accident and he should come home by the first plane. Knowing that her husband had a five-hour flight ahead of him, Jane could not bring herself to tell him their son was already dead. She remembers meeting her husband at the airport and watching him come down the stairs. He took one look at Jane and knew from her face it was serious. "Tony's gone," Jane told him. She does not remember any expression of emotion by her husband. They got into the car with two friends who had accompanied her to the airport, and Jane recalls nothing more. She has no conscious memory of anything she or her husband said for the next few days, even weeks. The funeral was on Sunday morning. Jane remembers going. She knew her mother and father had arrived from Florida, but that very awareness brought her intensified pain. Her parents stayed for a few days, but their grief so affected Jane that she was grateful when they left. It was a burden she could not assume. She could not bear their pain. "I couldn't look at their faces." Today, some seven years later, she has assumed a far greater burden. As director of the National Tay-Sachs Foundation, Jane works daily contributing to the well-being of parents who lose their children to that fatal disease—helping others survive.

For the memorial service held on March 4, 1973, for Carl Shapiro, who had died in a horseback riding accident, a tribute was written by his mother, Irma Shapiro. In part, it reads as follows:

> We had a son for twenty-three years. For the rest of our days, we will have to be content with the memory of those years. They were full years for Carl—and consequently, ours were full, too. In his comparatively short lifetime he achieved some distinctions. He was awarded a letter of commendation from the National Merit Scholarship program, which means he was in the top 2 percent of the country's graduating seniors.
>
> Like all parents, we were introduced to many new worlds

through our children, not all of them exactly what we would have chosen, but all contributing to our experience and our growth as individuals. And they were shared experiences, so that made them meaningful.

We are grateful for our lovely daughter, who is here with us from her home in Oregon. And grateful for our close relatives and dear friends, and the organizations which have meant so much to us during the years, especially the Ethical Society.

As the circle gets smaller, the circle gets more intense with feelings of love and devotion, and that is what we feel at this time, and this is what will help us in the difficult days ahead. What will also help us is the knowledge that brief as Carl's life was, he brought joy to many people and served many.

Nearly two thousand years ago, Plutarch, the Greek moralist, wrote this upon the death of his child:

"Should the sweet remembrances of those things which so delighted us when he was alive only afflict us now? Since he gave us so much pleasure while we had him, so we ought to cherish his memory, and make that memory a glad rather than sorrowful one.

"Let us not ungratefully accuse Fortune for what was given us, because we could not also have all that we desired. What we had and while we had it, was good, though now we have it no longer.

"Remember also how much good you still possess. Because one page of your book is blotted, do not forget all the other leaves whose reading is fair and whose pictures are beautiful. We should not be like a miser who never enjoys what he has, but only bewails what he loses."

While the above tribute reflects the feelings of love and devotion of a mother for her child, in the poem below, Irma speaks of the hurt:

I hurt
    Because I'll never hear his voice again,
    Because he'll never come home again,
    Because I'll never get a "hello" kiss,
    Because I'll never even get a nasty word.

I hurt
> Because I miss
>> His presence,
>> His expanded knowledge,
>> His sagacity,
>> His argumentativeness,
>> His stubbornness,
>> His handsome face,
>> His piercing eyes,
>> His tall, strong body.

I hurt
> Because I can't talk about
>> The experiences we had together,
>> The pains we suffered,
>> The joys that replaced the pains,
>> The baby things, so fun-filled,
>> The growing-up things, so poignant,
>> The adult things, so bewildering.

I hurt, I hurt!

In the early morning of March 14, 1981, Abe and Judy Malawski were sleeping in the upstairs bedroom of their home. Their younger son, Steven, seventeen, was also asleep. Their older son, Harvey, age nineteen, was away at college. At 4:30 A.M. there was a ring at the front door. Judy woke up first and told her husband the doorbell was ringing. Abe tells what happened next. "I went downstairs, and when I saw two state troopers, I didn't know what to think. They asked me if I was Abraham Malawski, and I said yes. Then they asked, 'Do you have a son, Harvey?' I nodded my head yes. And then they told me, 'Your son has been involved in a fatal accident.' My wife had come downstairs and started screaming. She began to hit the state trooper on the chest. She kept shouting, 'It's not true. It's not true.' She continued pounding away at the trooper. My other son came down and fell apart on the stairs when he heard my wife crying and yelling, 'My baby, my baby.' " In later weeks and months, while driving to work, Abe was to relive that scene many times. He kept remembering those early images. "My wife is all of five feet. The state trooper was over six feet tall. I keep seeing her hitting him and hearing her saying, 'It's not true. Tell me it's not true.' "

After a close friend and other family members were summoned, Abe was in a complete fog. "A friend took care of the funeral arrangements because he didn't want me to have to handle that." Another friend picked up Abe's in-laws, who came in from Florida. During the next seven days the family observed the tradition of sitting *shiva* in their home. Friends brought in food, but Abe doesn't remember who came or who went. The house was full of people. Abe does recall that most of the kids who went to school with Harvey came to pay their respects. "These kids seemed to feel it the most. You could see it in their faces. They would grab us and hold us, but I don't know what they said to us. I had also been involved with the Boy Scouts because of my sons. It seems that everyone connected with the troop came to the funeral. I was told that the cortege must have had about a hundred fifty cars. Cousins from Connecticut, Pennsylvania, and people from Boston came, and later I found out that members of Harvey's graduating class were at the funeral home to pay their last respects. But I knew nothing of any of this. I only saw people who came into the family room. The rest was just a blur. I just couldn't believe this was real."

Judith Haimes recalls her memories during the first days and weeks after her son's death. Her mind was foggy. She had the feeling of being "in and out," a sense of numbness. She remembers her husband, Allen, holding her, but she doesn't remember anything being real. She recalls that a nurse handed her a washcloth for her face, saying, "I am not only a nurse but a mother, too." Some months later a friend who was present just after Michael died noted that Judith kept saying to Allen, "We died. We just died." Judith remembers nothing of this.

She does vaguely remember being ushered out of the hospital into the car. As she looked up at the full moon, Judith was hit with the realization that many other full moons had taken their toll of children. Judith had always been the hopeless romantic, viewing the full moon as big and beautiful. But at that moment she wondered how many other parents were standing under this full moon and how many other children, like Michael, had died under this same full moon. "As I stood there, I realized for the first time in my entire life there were no words to describe the pain I felt. God never allowed man to put into words the kind of pain that is." The severity of Judith's pain was to continue for at least a week. It wasn't until the first week was over that she was aware of catching her breath, of being able to take a minute to go to the bathroom or to take a glass of water without excruciating pain gnawing at her.

Coming home from the hospital, Judith did not want to get out of the car. She did not want to go into the house. She knew if she went into the house, she would have to face the reality that this was not a dream, that Michael was really dead. At the same time she was filled with the dreadful thought that Michael *was* dead. "My pain, my sorrow, my suffering was for *me* because I was a mother and I had just lost my son. I had lost part of my own life. I felt a piece of myself had died at four forty-one that afternoon, a piece I knew would never come back again, ever." Ultimately Judith was convinced she should go into the house. "I remember clinging to Allen because although I felt this ungodly pain when I touched him, it was easier to carry a hundred pounds when you had someone sharing fifty pounds of it than it would be to carry the hundred pounds alone." During the next few days people came and went. Judith remembers them only vaguely. What she does remember is the *caring* of the people who came, the people who cried—for her and her husband, for her dead son, and for their own pain. What meant most to Judith and Allen during those moments was that the people there put Michael's parents first and themselves second.

There were moments, Judith remembers, when part of her was physically hungry. But she was unable to eat because she couldn't swallow anything. "In the back of my mind I would think: Michael can't eat. How can I eat? Michael is on a slab somewhere. He can't eat." During those moments Judith didn't know if she had to prove to Michael that by not eating, she was suffering enough for him or whether she had to prove this to herself.

Judith did not wish to go to the funeral or to the services. She did not want to see her son buried. "I never saw my son dead. When he died, I did not view his body. I am very grateful to this day that I did not because now when I picture Michael, I remember him kissing me good-bye, the way he would on any normal day." However, on the day of the funeral Judith did attend. She remembers the morning very well, from the time she left the doorway to her bedroom until she got into a chair by a front-room window. Suddenly she saw a car and was panic-stricken. "Oh, God, they are sending a car. And when that car comes, it will be over." After that shattering moment Judith remembers almost nothing. "From that point on I was in never-never land." Judith does not remember her husband and the rabbi taking her up to the Ark of the temple. She does not remember screaming. She does not remember refusing to throw a flower on her son's coffin in the cemetery. She does not remember any of these things others told her later. What she does remember is saying over and over again, "My Michael is gone. He is gone forever."

These early days of anguish are a period no parent gets through. It's just an existence of nonexistence. The beginning of survival comes later.

3 · The Pain of Grief

Ernie Freireich was away on business in Chicago, visiting an engineering firm. He had just returned from lunch when he received a telephone call from New York to drop everything and get back home. His seventeen-year-old son, Mark, had been in an automobile accident. "There was a terrible snowstorm, and it was hours before I could get out of Chicago. The delay was unbearable. I wanted to know how my son was." Ernie's boss met him at the airport and took him to the hospital. Ernie's wife, Joyce, was waiting for him there, and together they went into their son's room. "The sight was absolutely frightening. Tubes were in every part of his body. Initially we were told he was going to be all right. No sooner were we thanking God for that than we were told within twenty-four hours that Mark's situation had deteriorated. To go from the emotion of thinking he is all right and going to survive to that of total fear and despair is what they do in operas, not in real life." Mark was in a coma, which he remained in for four months until he died. His parents were devastated, watching him waste from 140 pounds to 67. But they also tried to convey hope to their son. Ernie remembers: "I would sing to him, talk to him, hoping that some miraculous spark would bring him out of the coma. I went through a period of bargaining, with anyone, anything— with God, with the devil. 'I'll trade you anything for my child's life.' But it was to no avail."

About eight months after the death of his son Ernie would go out into the woods and talk to God and ask, "Why?" Ernie recollects, "He was such a gentle boy. Where was God when it came to protecting my son? So then I began to talk to Mark. I asked him to give me a sign, just a little sign, and all the world

23

would come together again. He used to love cars and would always talk about a four-twenty-seven-cubic-inch engine. He used to doodle the number four-twenty-seven on anything and everything. So out here in the woods, talking to my son, I thought of that, and I said, 'Mark, just show me that number.' It was Sunday night, and I went to bed. When I went to work the next day, I kept looking for cars passing by to have the number four-twenty-seven, or a bus, looking everywhere for some sign. Nothing. I had not told my wife about this. I didn't know how she would feel about it. I remained silent and did not discuss it either with my wife or my two daughters, Deborah, eleven, or Jennifer, fourteen. The following Friday my wife and I came home after shopping at the supermarket. She told me Deborah was having a problem sleeping and had not slept well for the last five nights. Deborah kept hearing a voice she thought was Mark's. When she woke up, the voice kept telling her to look at the clock. When she did, the time was four twenty-seven. This happened for five consecutive nights. Each time Deborah looked at the clock it was four twenty-seven. On the sixth night I slept in Deborah's room, but there were no more voices."

Deborah was not alone in suffering through sleepless nights. Ernie remembers, "While Mark was in the coma, I would sob at night and my wife would get very angry. My crying implied certain conclusions other than 'He is going to be all right.' I had to sleep in a separate bed, where I could sob myself to sleep. I had to sob at night because society says, 'Don't lose control of yourself.' And I remembered my father saying, 'Big boys don't cry.' But what people are really saying is: 'Don't lose control because I can't cope with your demonstration.' So I developed a subconscious type of crying—the tears would be running down my face inside and no one could see them."

Jane Birnbaum's sixteen-year-old son, Tony Sakolsky, was killed in a car crash. For a long time thereafter Jane suffered from a great sense of guilt for his death. It was her normal habit to pick up her son after school. However, the family car was in the garage for service. Tony telephoned to say he had a lift from school to the garage and he would bring the car home. His father was out of town at the time, so Jane consented to Tony's request. But that concession cost her dearly, for she was whipped relentlessly by the sense of guilt for her son's death. "I always felt that if I had picked him up, it never would have happened. I believed this for a very long time."

Apart from the torture of this guilt, Jane was fearful she was losing her mind. She experienced "in and out" periods. She remembers the night she drove to the hospital where they told her Tony had died. "It was in a section of the hospital that was near the parking lot. I clearly remember driving up there. I remember the building. I remember walking in. For several months I couldn't go near that area, and for a while I wouldn't drive anywhere by myself. When I finally did, I drove past that section of town. I was coming along the road and the building *wasn't there. It was gone!* I thought to myself: You know something, you are losing your mind! I know you were here. I know you were in that building. Pinch yourself! Maybe Tony is home. Maybe he is alive. Maybe you never walked into that building. Maybe it never happened. Could it be?" Jane went through this incredible fantasy only to learn later that the building had been torn down right after the accident. "But for that brief segment of time I allowed myself to think that all this had never really happened." These types of fantasies began to occur frequently. If Jane left the house for more than an hour, when she came back, she expected to find everything as it had been before Tony died, as though nothing had changed. Coming back to the house at night and seeing the lights on, she would think: "He is going to be there when I get home. This just can't have happened!" Jane is not alone, for many parents have experienced these same types of fantasies. In some instances perhaps they preserve sanity.

Several months after the death of her son Jane knew she had to seek professional help. She and her husband were not communicating. She had to reach out to somebody. Jane found a doctor to help her but remembers little of going to the doctor's office either on the initial visit or during subsequent ones. Yet she knows she went. She remembers spottily the drive to his office and parking the car. Vaguely she recalls once entering the doctor's office and commenting on the smell of smoke. Jane remembers almost nothing of what was discussed while she was in treatment for six months to a year after her son's death. The only conversation she does recall is the doctor urging her to see friends. She followed his advice and began to invite people to her home. Ten people for dinner. Twelve people for dinner. This busied her with cooking, with preparations. It was a start to a way back.

In 1947 Maria and Nicolo Orlando were a very happy couple. They had a beautiful daughter, and now God had blessed them with a son. The baby was fine until the second month. The infant's head wouldn't lie properly, and his muscular movement was impaired. At the hospital doctors said it was an unusual case and wanted to study it further. It became increasingly difficult for the baby to swallow, and Maria took careful precautions during feeding time. When he was five months old, however, he choked on an egg and couldn't swallow it. Maria's aunt was present and attempted mouth-to-mouth resuscitation, but to no avail. The baby died in Maria's arms on Columbus Day, a day she would remember all her life.

After the funeral Maria was desolate. She would see a pregnant woman and become jealous because she was going to have a child. She wanted desperately to have more children of her own. But she was apprehensive, wondering if another child would suffer as this infant had. After a time Maria did become pregnant again, and ultimately she gave birth to a second son. Everything was fine for the first month. Then the same problems arose. The baby's head would not lie properly, and muscles did not develop in some parts of his body. At six months of age the infant caught cold. The doctors diagnosed the problem as bronchitis, and the baby was hospitalized. When Maria went to the hospital the second day, the baby wasn't there. "I found an empty room, just a crib. My son had died just a short time before I arrived. I was told the baby had been taken to the morgue, but I insisted on seeing him. The nurse hugged me and comforted me and said she would take me to see my baby. When I saw him, it was as if he were sleeping; he was such a beautiful baby."

Months later Maria found herself pregnant again. The doctors, after the death of the second son, wanted her to abort the child. Maria told them she had a healthy daughter and refused. "But I was very concerned. I did not want to make a baby suffer. However, I had a daughter who was healthy, and I hoped this child would be, too. I prayed the baby would survive." Maria gave birth to a husky boy of nine pounds. Although she was happy and the infant seemed frisky, Maria worried. The first month would tell. If only he survived that first month. Maria developed a tremble, fearful of a recurrence of what had happened to her first two sons. She began to suffer from severe stomach pain. After the second month the baby began kicking in a normal fashion. When Maria saw he was swallowing and moving properly, her sickness went away and she ceased trembling. Today, many years later, Maria comments, "After my third son and then my second daughter, my illness disappeared, but you never forget."

Abe Malawski and his wife were trying to find ways to relieve their agonizing pain. They began to go out for dinner with his brother and sister-in-law. They would always go to a small, quiet place because Judy had become sensitive to noise and crowds. One night they were joined by another couple, who were friends of Abe's brother. On the way back from the restaurant Abe and Judy stopped at the couple's house for coffee. Abe relaxed on a recliner. He was joined by the couple's younger son, thirteen, who showed Abe his recent Bar Mitzvah pictures. As they were looking at the pictures, the boy turned to Abe and asked, "How many children do you have?"

Abe swallowed hard. The question hit him between the eyes. He looked at the boy sitting beside him and said, "I *had* two sons."

The boy inquired, "Oh, you mean one got married?"

Abe paused for a moment and then replied, "No, one died." Abe felt the pain of this young boy as well as his own. "The kid swallowed just as hard as I did and said, 'I'm very sorry.' And being a very sensitive child, he had the presence of mind to change the subject."

This was the first time Abe had been exposed to the question "How many children do you have?" since his son's death. His reactions were the same as they had been to the first holiday after Harvey died. "The first time is the worst time, whether it's your first party, the first holiday, or the first birthday. You count the days before their arrival like a convict counting down before going to the electric chair: nine, eight, seven, six. Then the date of the anniversary comes. You wake up and go through the motions. When the next day comes, you realize the anniversary date passed somehow, that this is the day after and you are still alive."

The holidays were particularly painful for Abe, Judy, and their son, Steven. "Writing New Year cards for the first time was horrible. Signing the cards from the three of us instead of the four of us brought everything back in a different intensity. Then I just became numb and continued to write automatically. It's like a circle divided into four. The circle is not complete anymore. The continuity is not there anymore in whatever you do. It's like everything else. The first time for anything is the hardest. The second and third times are bad, and then you have experienced it. You have at least already gone through the 'first' time."

Abe feels there are moods every bereaved parent goes through. "You wonder: Am I normal? Whatever that may mean. You are trying to survive. You are trying to keep from drowning. Then, when you meet other couples who have had the same experience, you learn you are not the only one drowning. Everyone else is drowning and acting in a different way, trying to make it. I don't think we could have known or learned this if it had not been for the group meetings we attended. So I guess it is a combination of several things: the fact that we went to The Compassionate Friends, that we are going to group therapy at Family Services, hearing other couples talk. We learn about their moods. Then we find out we are not strange. We learn that sometimes by not being an active participant with your feelings, you are also making a statement. And it is not necessarily a bad one. You are saying, 'I am not ready.' Or you are saying, 'I hurt so much I cannot bear the thought of doing something about it.' Or you are simply saying, 'Give me time.' "

Abe believes his emotional makeup enables him to deal better with his loss. "Sometimes I break down. I cry. And then I continue whatever it is I am doing. It's like children who learn to walk. They fall down. But they stand up and they walk. And they fall down again and stand up. It's a constant falling down until finally they are able to control themselves and stay up. I tend to think bereavement is pretty much the same way."

Abe describes what it was like to attend a meeting of a peer group: "When we went to The Compassionate Friends for the very first time, about seven weeks after Harvey passed away, there were probably fifty or sixty people there. All meetings start the same way. The chairperson tells everyone why she is there, and then everyone continues all around the room. When it came to us, Judy couldn't talk, so I introduced us and told the people gathered why we were there. Let me tell you that it is the hardest thing to do next to losing your child. I couldn't talk. I stammered. I cried. I mumbled. I stumbled. But finally, I got it out. Every meeting starts like this. This group helped me a lot, so much so that now, ten months later, I go on with the job of being alive and trying to put myself together as best I can. One of the ways I knew I was progressing in my sorrow and despair was that I used the introductions at the meetings as a guiding beacon. By this I mean that at the second meeting I was able to introduce ourselves without stammering and choking. I did cry, but it was easier. At the third meeting I cried less and at the last one I went to, on New Year's Day, eleven months later, I did not cry. Grieving is a process whereby you must say over and over again why you are grieving. And slowly but surely, as time goes on, you purge yourself of all that pent-up feeling and emotion that are killing you. You know you must go on because you have no choice. Or rather, the alternatives are infinitely worse. So actually you do not have a good choice. Time is the best healer. Time and other grieving parents, because one supports the other, without your actually being aware of doing it."

Barbara Davis, whose son was murdered in a house robbery, described a type of free-floating guilt. "It isn't right for parents to survive their children. It's not natural." There were periods of anger, hopelessness, and seemingly endless grief. Because their house was being examined by police for clues to the murder of their son, Barbara and Sid remained at the home of neighbors for several nights. "For a long while every time I went into a bathroom I would cry. Isn't it terrible to think of your son at a time like that? When I was at our neighbor's house during those first few days, I would go to the bathroom when I felt like letting loose and crying, and it became the place I could be alone and shed my tears." There were also moments when guards were relaxed momentarily and a laugh was provoked by a television comic. "You would find yourself chuckling, and then you would say, 'My God, how can I laugh?' But eventually you accept yourself and you do."

Barbara and her husband found the trick was to make the

time go by fast. They visited friends, went to relatives, to neighbors' homes, were very restless. This running is a familiar experience to bereaved parents. If you run fast enough, you won't have to remember. The first six months after their son was murdered consisted of frantic activity, for these were months fraught with depression. Barbara and Sid theorized if they didn't go to bed too early, they would not get up early. One week after the death of her son Barbara went back to work. She cried going and coming, but for the most part she was able to work. Barbara is a visiting nurse and was geared to working with families, rather than with patients in a hospital. In continuing to help others, especially in a family setting, she was also able to help herself.

Angela and Peter Purpura also ran. And kept running. Every night they would go out of the house, seeking the same kind of relief Barbara and Sid Davis sought: the relief that moving, moving, would in some way not allow time to freeze in the agonizing present. That somehow moving would push the clock forward to some future time when grief would not exist. When pain would not exist. When anguish was no more. A time void of thoughts of a dead child.

Angela says on some days she is more depressed than others. Some require more effort. This is especially true of shopping days. Many parents have traumatic experiences in what used to be "normal" activities, such as going to the supermarket. "Do you know I always wear sunglasses to the supermarket, even in the winter," Angela states. "I actually brace myself with list in hand and charge through the aisles, looking straight ahead." While it seems like such a simple chore to go to the supermarket, Angela, like many other parents, is faced with so many of her child's favorite foods—foods Cassandra can never have again. Also, the trip to the store means one risks running into other mothers. "There are those who, in fact, hide around the aisle when they see me coming, or mutter hello and quickly move on. They don't know what to say. And I really don't want to hear them either." Her daughter Cassandra was an integral part of their family. Without her to share the remaining years, there will always be an emptiness. For Angela, the memories have been the most difficult aspect of her grief. With the memories comes the sheer longing for her child. The happy memories intensify the loss she feels. The sad memories of her illness and the deterioration Cassandra experienced during her three-month struggle with cancer are thoughts Angela continues to push to the depths of her mind. To dwell on these, she feels, would surely destroy what she is trying to build again. No bereaved parent should go back that far.

Many have asked Angela, "Aren't you angry with God?" She replies, "What would it accomplish? Does anger ever accomplish anything positive?" Nevertheless, Angela was angry. Not with any specific focus, but she was angry with life. "Why did this tragedy strike our family? Cassandra, who suffered through her illness, we struggling with helping her through it with the least possible fear and pain both physically and emotionally. And now we are left to pick up the pieces of our lives that were so shattered." In reality, Angela believes they will never know the *why.* For some questions there are no answers. "These questions are best not asked," Angela thinks.

During the second winter without her daughter a former friend contacted Angela. The friend's son had been injured in a sledding accident. The boy required many stitches in his head. Totally insensitive to the anguish she was causing Angela, the woman kept repeating that God must have loved her a great deal to have spared her son's life. Angela bitterly thought: Was that the answer to my *why?*

Then there are grievances against those who said all the wrong things or did not do what they should have during Cassandra's illness, at her death, and later in reaction to her parents' grief. "I have turned from many people because I am totally disinterested and incapable of making excuses for them," Angela comments. Such as the grandfather who visited only once during Cassandra's illness, her uncles, who never knew her or asked about her when she was dying, the classmate who laughed when Cassandra proudly announced she was able to ride a tricycle when she was so physically impaired, the schoolteacher who wore jeans to the wake, the parent at school who thought the Purpuras were "bonkers" for not having chosen radiation, even though it did not afford any hope, the relative who criticized them for burying Cassandra with a gold ring, stating if the undertakers didn't steal it, certainly the gravediggers would.

One week after Cassandra died, the mother of one of her classmates called to invite Angela to lunch. The mother asked her how she was doing. When Angela replied, "Not so well," the mother asked what was wrong. Indeed, her child dead only one week, what could possibly be wrong? The woman, who was class mother, indicated the class would like to dedicate something in Cassandra's memory. Angela suggested that planting a tree on the campus would be a lovely idea. "But nothing was ever dedicated. And it hurts a lot." Angela's surviving daughter, Cara, is now in the third grade, the last grade Cassandra reached. She's in the same room that Cassandra was in, with the same teachers. It is difficult for Angela to communicate with the faculty, and she often wonders if she is overly sensitive. But, she asks, "Did they really appreciate Cassandra and the value she placed on school?"

Angela is not sure anger or sheer rage can stand alone. With them come the companions of depression and hurt. All the injustices of her past life suddenly become monumental: her sense of being unloved as a child, the nonexistence of family unity during those years before she had a family of her own; finally, the total lack of recognition of Angela as a person. All that, coupled with losing her little girl, played havoc with Angela and took its toll on the assessment she made of herself.

She believes the grief that besets a bereaved parent cannot adequately be put into words. That grief is like an umbrella, spanning many other fears and anxieties that consume bereaved parents. There is an underlying worry that there may be no tomorrow. As a group grieving parents no longer fear death. "After all, if our children can endure it, so can we." The time factor gnaws at the grieving parent. "How much time do we have left with our surviving children? How much time do we have left with our spouse? How much time do we have left?" Often this fear works as an impetus to enable parents to accomplish the most difficult tasks, but there are other times it renders them immobile. Just as fear can destroy the future, living with guilt related to the past can mar what is left to parents. "If only I had loved her differently. Could I have loved her more? If only I had fed her differently." These thoughts tormented Angela. Yet she had prepared all fresh foods, no preservatives, no additives, whole wheat products, homemade bread. At age eight years and ten months, Cassandra never had a cavity. Angela's husband, Peter, looks at it in a more positive vein. He asked Angela to consider how her care of Cassandra may have lengthened her life, allowing her to reach the age of eight.

The psychotherapist Angela and Peter visited, prior to and after their daughter's death, took the position that all illnesses are psychogenic in origin. "Therefore," Angela remembers, "he held to the belief that Cassandra's brain tumor was caused by the emotional irritants in her environment. Both Peter and I suffered severe feelings of guilt. Later Peter took it more philosophically, but my guilt remained for a long time."

Angela and Peter have since gone on to become the chairpersons of the Long Island, New York, chapter of The Compassionate Friends. From that post they have observed and listened to other bereaved parents' experiences with counselors. Angela offers some insight to others seeking to counsel the bereaved: "The helping professionals should be made aware of what to look for in bereaved parents. The feedback from members who sought professional help before coming to The Compassionate Friends has indicated, one, that the professionals lack knowledge of what is normal behavior for bereaved parents and frequently interpret grief reactions as emotional disturbances and two, too often professionals place a time limit on grief and take the position 'Isn't it time you got over this?' It is not the length of time that has passed, but how that time has been utilized. I have talked with, met with, and received mail from many bereaved parents whose children died three, five, and even fifteen or twenty years ago, and their loss appears to have occurred just recently. They have had no one with whom they could work through their grief, no one to listen to them, no one who understood their problems." Angela continues: "Parents are so vulnerable at a time like this. They should look carefully at whom to go into treatment with or whether to go into treatment at all. Many times parents just want to verify that they are not crazy."

Angela also comments on the pain suffered by adoptive and stepparents: "Adoptive parents and stepparents grieve too. It is not uncommon for non-biological parents to seek help through TCF. Many do not make their biological status known to other members however. This issue seems a private matter for, in fact, depending upon the length of their parenting a deceased child and the quality of that relationship, their pain is the pain experienced by natural parents. To make any distinction would be saying in effect, 'My pain is greater than yours.' Although this may be disputed between the couples themselves, how useless and irrelevant to focus anyone's grief on that plane. Adoptive and stepparents vary in their expression of pain, their sense of loss, and their ability to be supportive of their spouse, as do natural parents. What appears to be a more pertinent issue is if the deceased child had never been accepted by the step or adoptive parent as their own or if the bereaved parent remarries and is grieving a child their new spouse never knew."

Peter, himself a psychoanalyst, offers an indication to other bereaved parents of when counseling might be needed: "When should a therapist be consulted? When there is no one to talk to or to be with to help you go through the pain. In this instance pain is part of the growth and repair of recovering from a devastating loss. That process cannot be done totally alone. If there is no friend or family member to help, then a counselor could fill that void. Too, if there are serious emotional problems that don't allow the grief process to take place, a counselor may help. The grief process basically is resurrecting all the expectations that you had of the dead person and dealing with the pain that those expectations will never be. There will never again be a holding, a touching, seeing them for a holiday, and the pain of disconnecting must be dealt with. Wakes, sitting *shiva,* and other traditional practices help focus the reality of the death as well as provide others to listen. However, grief goes on after these brief periods—for at least a year. In the case of the death of a child, two years or more are typical periods for grieving with periods of grief for many years thereafter."

Peter expresses the feeling that before Cassandra died, they had dealt with an expanding life. His professional practice was going well. They had children. Angela was active and doing things. With Cassandra's death their life contracted sharply. "That was a whole shift in what life is all about, what you can expect from it. That comes for a lot of people later, when your body starts giving you trouble. It was an introduction to the whole idea that life is not an ongoing positive process. At some point it involves contracting and losing things." The enormous sense of contraction hasn't changed for Peter. Things he once was very excited about and were important to him don't mean much anymore. "There's an edge to everything." However, Angela and Peter are trying very hard to look to the needs of their younger surviving child, who doesn't even remember what Christmas was like. "The traditional Christmas is too painful," Angela states. "You have to do things differently from before. There is too much reliving otherwise. It is important to change things from the way they were. They can never be the same. Your child will not be there." The first two Christmases after Cassandra died, Angela, Peter, and their surviving daughter, Cara, went to Barbados. There was nothing Christmaslike in that tropical environment. They are planning the next Christmas for Cara. They won't have caroling or the neighbors to their home, but they will invite a sister and other bereaved parents who have older children. They want to have some sense of tradition for their younger daughter.

Peter, too, has expressed his feelings of anger and hurt:

"Anger? Have I been angry about Cassandra's death? Angry with whom: God, Angela, myself? I guess I have been angry. There are times I am unbearable, and I am not sure why. I guess it is because of Cassandra's death.

"I have been thankful I have been spared the anger and hurt of asking why she died. That question I have not tortured myself with. I know there is no answer, and we must accept the fact of our child's death and never know why she died. There is no difference if it was illness, accident, suicide, or murder; the real *why?* we will never know. To ask this is of no value or help. As soon as we can help ourselves, it is best to stop asking for it can be a terrible source of anguish and serves only to pain us.

"The helplessness of it all is so painful, so strange. Not to be able to do anything, nothing at all! How debilitating that is; we were so strong, so effective before this. Now with our own child we are helpless? It cannot be, but it is. She is dead! And we are alive.

"It is so hard even to be with Cara at times. She reminds me of her missing sister, just by her presence. At times I am so short with her. It is hard to take her to the playground. She asked once, and my heart sank. I went with Cassandra when she was ill. She could barely walk, and I took her. Oh, my God, Cara is on the monkey bars just like Cassandra. I can't stand it. Be quiet! It is not fair; she is yours, too. Just a child; she has a right to play, to your attention and love. But it never hurt like this. Before it was never so hard or full of painful memories that turn so easily to *anger!*"

The pain and grief caused by the death of a child are a completely shattering experience—inconceivable, unnatural. There is no comfort. No consolation. The despair and torment devastates parents who look not for solace—only for relief from the unbearable pain. Poet Edna St. Vincent Millay captures the feeling with uncanny perception:

> Time does not bring relief.
> You all have lied who told me
> time would ease me of my pain. . . .

Judith Haimes describes how people kept coming to her and saying, "Time will make it better. Time will ease the pain." She has learned, however, time doesn't do any of those things. "We all have believed that time heals all wounds. We all have said it: 'In time you will feel better.'" Judith found that time helped only to control the situation. "Time helps you adjust to the things around you. Time does not make the pain go away. The pain is still acute months, years later. The only difference is that we are capable of adjusting and learning to live with it. You learn to do things differently."

Months after the death of her son Michael, Judith continued to receive an outpouring of sympathy from the people around her. She found herself wallowing in it—playing the role of just what was expected of her. "Oh, my God, this poor thing. She is suffering so badly," they would say. Judith found it was as if people were making excuses for her grief—that it was all right for her to suffer. Soon she began to realize she was very vulnerable to these suggestions and felt they were making her weak. She was sinking very rapidly. "It is *so easy* to feel sorry for yourself when you are in pain. And it is *so very hard* to pull yourself together when you don't want to live. People meant well, and I am very, very grateful they were there. But I had to start separating myself from those who would say, 'Oh, poor baby.' "

Judith felt that if she had to live, and she knew she must, she had to start. She had to stop pulling her husband and their surviving children down. "I had to stop allowing my oldest daughter to be stronger and better than her mother. I had to give her an example to live up to. I had to give my other sons the mother that Michael had. I had to give my husband the wife he deserved." In order to pull herself up, Judith had to wipe the slate clean. She literally had to start all over again. She began to do things for herself rather than allow others to do them for her. She eliminated those friends and relatives around her who she felt were keeping her weak. Although she knew they meant well, she stopped seeing the people who would continue to say, "Hello, you poor baby. How much you are suffering! Why don't you rest? Don't do this. Don't do that. It doesn't matter." Judith didn't want to receive any more telephone calls that started out "Hello, how are you? Don't say how fine you are. I know how the pain is." After weeks and months of hearing how much she was suffering, Judith realized how much she *was* really suffering. She didn't want to get up in the morning. She couldn't face the day. She didn't want to fix her hair or cook supper.

Then one day Judith decided, "I will always love Michael. I will always feel Michael close to me. I will always miss him. But I need time alone to be myself. I need time to be strong for my husband and my other children." So now in the morning, when she really wants to stay in bed and cover her head and not face the pain of the day, Judith gets up. She makes breakfast for her children and talks to them. She takes long walks with them, and they watch the birds and look at the trees. She feels she is a mother again.

Ellen Uhl was haunted by images following the death of her son Danny: seeing a little boy in the subway wearing a Yankee

T-shirt, hearing a basketball bounce, passing the high school on the way home from work. "I would remember the times when he was a baby, whereas before I couldn't seem to remember them when he was living." Ellen found things that never bothered her before now affected her severely. She can no longer bear the chatter of meaningless talk, for example. "Most of our waking hours are spent parroting the rest of the world. Words like 'Well, it looks like it's going to rain tomorrow' or 'That's what makes the world go round.' " Work was often a test of endurance for Ellen. After a loss of weight some of the girls in the office commented, "Oh, Ellen, how do you keep such a trim figure?" Ellen wanted to scream, "Don't you know my son is dead? How can I eat with my son in the ground?" Why do they ask such insensitive questions? she wonders. "If only they could crawl into my brain and feel my agony." Her thoughts keep going back to her son's pain. She had visions of him with his chest hurting. She kept thinking back to those five awful days before he died, not knowing if her son would have brain damage or if an amputation would be required. Although her world has caved in, Ellen still goes to work, still tries to find a way to be a mother to her surviving son. Initially she resented it when her older son wore some of Danny's clothes. Later she realized he only had a need to be close to his brother in some way. He was hurting, too. Often there were moments when Ellen wanted to hide under the pillow. "No, no. I cannot face another day." But Ellen found help in facing those days through a self-help group of other bereaved parents. Her mother, Ethel—the grandmother who had helped rear Danny since he was a small child—also participated in this peer group. At first she was reluctant to do so, but she has found it a help. Ethel knows her life will never be the same. But she remains active in women's groups, workshops, choral group. "They offer a lot," she believes.

Doris Young recalls the first days and weeks after the drowning of her young son. She saw people coming and going but was in a state of shock. She was doing things routinely but was not aware of doing them. For the next couple of months Doris couldn't get out of the chair. Her mother-in-law had to care for her surviving small children because Doris just wasn't capable of doing so. She was not able to focus on anything except excruciating, mesmerizing pain. As the months passed, Doris wasn't able to talk to anyone—not even her best friend. Then she began to experience hostile feelings toward everyone. Friends came and said the necessary things. But she wanted to strike out, to ask, "How do you know? How do you know about what I am feeling?" Six months later she moved away from the neighborhood. Doris was angry with God and asked, "How did God let this happen? Why would God do this to me? I never mistreated anyone. I have been a good person. Why?" She began to examine herself for reasons and the hostility toward God and everyone else grew. The cry *why?* is the cry of pain that every bereaved parent suffers. Since no answer is forthcoming, concerned friends and family members can only remain near, offering love and expressions of caring.

When she began to think of suicide, Doris knew she had to get help because her remaining children needed her. An elderly neighbor who had also lost a child urged her not to be afraid to seek guidance, and for the next four months Doris was under psychiatric care. Her feelings of guilt were overwhelming. "If only I had looked behind me. If I had spent more time with him. If I had gone to the store later." These many years later Doris doesn't blame herself anymore. There are still moments of pain—particularly during holidays, on her son's birthday, or when she hears news or reads of another child who has died. But Doris considers herself a survivor and strives hard to make holidays happy ones for her remaining children.

At the time of her son's death in 1972 Doris had been separated from her husband. She subsequently divorced and remarried. She was elated to find herself pregnant once more, thinking the new baby was being sent as a replacement for her dead child. However, the baby was stillborn, and Doris suffered the pain of yet another loss. Drawing on inner resources, she knew from experience the secret to survival was to keep busy, to put her children ahead of herself. In her initial grief after her eight-year-old son had died, Doris remained at home. Her doctor urged her to get a job and return to work. Doris feels this proved to be her salvation. It necessitated her taking a bus. It made her aware she needed car fare to get on that bus. And once off that bus, she had a destination other than a home without her son in it.

The shock impact of a child's death leaves parents with one of the cruelest of all emotions—the total sense of powerlessness. The sheer frustration at not being able to control something so vital to parents—the ability to protect a child—drags them to the depths of despair. One mother who felt the impact of such a shock was Ruth Redemann, who lost her entire family in one fell swoop. On a bright Labor Day weekend Ruth's only daughter, son-in-law, two grandchildren, and the family dog got into the car for an outing from which they never returned. They all were killed in a car accident. When Ruth was asked how she survived such a tragedy—to lose her only child, her only grandchildren—she replied, "I had to become my own psychiatrist and my own counselor. Many times I would sit and watch television, but a girl in the commercial would look like my daughter. So I had to walk away from it because I would be so upset. Once, while I was lunching with a neighbor, she began to talk about how adorable her grandchildren were when visiting with her the previous day. I had to get up and leave. I went to another friend's house nearby and just began to scream. I simply couldn't understand how anyone could be so cruel as to talk about her grandchildren in front of me."

To Ruth, everything was a reminder. Even hearing the familiar bark of a dog would evoke tears. "I began to realize in time that no amount of crying would ever bring them back.

While there were moments I wanted to jump off the roof, and a time when I wanted to run to the graves and pull my children out, I knew I had to face the reality that I would never see them again, that nothing I could do would return them to me." Ruth was no stranger to grief; her mother and husband had died earlier, compounding her sense of "aloneness" in her grief over the loss of all her children. "My doctor urged me to go back to work, and I did after six weeks. While it was a salvation in many ways, there were unspeakably harsh facts I had to face. People were not interested in death. They were interested in life and consumed with interest in material aspects, like how much money was I going to get from the accident."* As if any money could compensate for such a loss! While many of her co-workers expressed sympathetic comments, the interest of others centered on what Ruth would do with money she got from the insurance company. Overlooked completely was the devastation she felt as the result of such great insensitivity. After ten years the sense of loss is still there, but Ruth tries to remove it from her mind by occupying herself with various activities, taking walks, going to bingo, being with a friend. She feels the most important thing she can convey to bereaved parents is: Force yourself to get out of the house, to walk, to talk to yourself—to be your own best friend.

Would that a parent's grief could be buried with the child. Since it cannot be, it is vital to find ways of coping. While certain approaches to combating grief may not work for some, the same approaches may offer solutions to others seeking to diminish pain and sorrow. The most difficult hurdle is the initial attempt to reenter a world that can never be the same.

---

*The irony was that Mrs. Redemann collected no insurance money.

4 · Babies Die, Too

The grief of young parents who lose a child shortly after birth is heartbreaking. About 48,000 infants die in this way annually in the United States alone. This does not include stillborns. Until recently most hospitals dealt ineptly with the anguish of the couples. Today, however, there are many new approaches for helping young grief-stricken parents. One such support group for those parents whose infants had died was formed at St. John's Hospital in Springfield, Illinois. It is called SHARE—and that is exactly what the bereaved parents do. They offer each other relief by ventilating their sorrow, their pain. Pent-up feelings of anger and resentment can be spoken aloud in the presence of others who have suffered the same pain. There are about 150 similar groups around the country, but St. John's was one of the first to function within a hospital.

Sue and Jerry Matthews' daughter, Elizabeth, was born after an emergency Caesarean was performed. The baby was later transferred to St. John's Hospital and placed in the High Risk Center there. A week later, when learning her baby would not survive, Sue began to weep, "I never even got to rock her." The poignant statement of this young mother so touched the hospital staff they scurried about and produced a rocking chair. Twenty minutes later a grateful parent was able to say, "I rocked my child into the arms of God."

Elizabeth's parents suffered an acute awareness of their child's struggling and suffering. Sue recalls the treatment Elizabeth received prior to her transfer to St. John's: "An IV was put into the baby's artery instead of the vein, and our baby lost the use of her arm." The arm could not be removed, and the two devastated parents had to endure the agony of watching little Elizabeth's arm turn brown and wither. Sue describes what happened and her emotional reactions, "The artery had shut down, and they couldn't get circulation going again in the arm. And we watched our little girl struggle to live. But she did have spontaneous movement. She looked for me and she would hold my finger. When she died, we had such a strong feeling that she was with God and wasn't struggling anymore."

Sue and Jerry had two surviving children. When Kara, their six-year-old daughter, was told her sister had died, she said, "Elizabeth is the first one in our family to see Jesus." When Jeremy, their three-year-old son, saw that Sue was crying, he climbed up onto her lap and said, "I will kiss it, and it will go away. I will make it well." But nothing could make it well.

It took three months before Sue could count on herself not to fall apart. She thought she was having a nervous breakdown. She suffered from insomnia, and when she did sleep, she had terrible nightmares. "At three-thirty A.M., I woke up and tried to count sheep, but soon they turned into little babies instead of sheep." She became frightened of her feelings and told her husband, "I am getting to a place I may not be able to get back from." She was suffering from physical exhaustion and grieving. Sue becomes furious with people who say, "Well, it was just an infant. It lived just a few days." She has strong feelings about parents who try to measure grief by the age of a child. "Some say, 'She can't understand what I feel because her baby didn't live and mine did.' Others say, 'Oh, well, her child was just a baby and not a grown child and it isn't the same.' A baby is a baby, and that child is your child regardless of its age. Grief is grief. I don't care if the child is twenty years old or one day old. If that baby is loved and wanted, that is where your heart is, and the loss is tremendous."

Sue says she will never forget what happened. "I asked the Lord, 'Take as much of it as you can without letting me forget.' I don't ever want to forget her. But you have to live. You either live with it or die. There are people who choose that way. In one way or another they choose not to live. It is social suicide and can end a marriage. I had a difficult time with my own parents. I felt they didn't understand she was my baby. But even if she was fifteen inches long and just two pounds, she was still my little girl—and she died."

Sue's mother-in-law came for a week to help after the baby died, and then her mother came for several days. Sue sat and rocked and cried a lot. Gradually she worked into things. She went to church. She resumed going to class. Every now and then the children were confused because she cried so much. Kara, a very intelligent little girl, asked questions like "How big were her hands?" After a lot of questioning by her daughter, Sue said she couldn't answer any more questions. When her son, Jeremy, asked about the baby, Sue told him, "She is with Jesus, and we won't see her for a long time, but one day we will."

While Sue says she is no longer the same person she was, she has come to terms with a lot of things. "There is no forgetting. You never are the same again, but I would say I have recovered as much as I can. With love and the Lord Himself, I think there is a lot of hope. I always thought I was a strong person, but I almost went over the line. I looked at members of the SHARE group who were here for three years. I would look at them and realize they had come from where I was and I would find a great deal of hope that someday I would be better the way they were. It was a hope—a light at the end of the tunnel."

Sue tells of her thoughts about attending meetings at SHARE. "Often we have a program dealing with some aspect of loss. Often we just talk. We get out all the feelings of anger at hospitals, doctors, or family members. Jealousies—everyone is pregnant when your baby dies. It is so good to know that these feelings are common. I realized I didn't have to feel guilty about not wanting to look at my friends' babies. It was good for me to be able to see parents who had experienced loss several years before and who said, 'My baby(ies) died. . . .' I *knew* that someday I would be able to deal with it better. We have fun together, too. It's not just tears. There is also laughter and joy. It's almost like finding a lot of best friends. *Some* people do understand. People were willing to share their time with me, and *they did* understand. It's wonderful to have a place to go where I can talk about my baby. No one looks off into the distance when I say Elizabeth's name. No one changes the subject. People care. Most of us really do feel that time spent at SHARE is time spent with our babies."

In speaking with Sister Jane Marie Lamb of the SHARE group at St. John's one night, Sue was told there was a letter for her at the office. "When Ann Landers mentioned SHARE in her column, we received five hundred letters the first week. I took seven letters to respond to and spent eight hours writing them instead of baking, et cetera. But it was worth it. The first letter that came back, which is the one Sister Jane Marie called me about, said, 'Thank you so much for the letter. It was my Christmas present.' This response from a bereaved mother was a blessing to me in that I know our loss has not been for nothing."

Sue states that time involved in the resolution of grief is variable. Everyone has his or her own calendar, and there can be no measurement of time.

Sandy and Mike Branham were thrilled at the prospect of being parents. They were happily anticipating the arrival of their first child. Suddenly, when Sandy was five months pregnant, she went into labor. It was their wedding anniversary. Twin boys, Randy and Richard, were born on February 15, 1978. But hours later the children died. Mike proudly recalls, "Randy was thirteen ounces and nine and a half inches long, and Richard was twelve ounces and nine inches long."

As Mike waited for word, the doctor came out to see him.

Wishing to prepare Mike for what had happened, the doctor told him his wife was all right, but his sons were dead. The doctor left, and Mike went in to see the children. When he did, one of the twins drew a breath, and it frightened the wits out of Mike. What happened then was a nightmare to him. At least one of his sons was alive, and the staff didn't seem to know this. Mike ran to a nearby nurse, who assured him the children were not going to survive. The doctor, apparently believing the children would soon be dead, had been trying to protect Mike by preparing him, Mike feels. "When I saw my son take a breath, I felt there was something the doctors or nurses should be doing that they weren't. You are so vulnerable at a time like that. Later I realized the doctor was trying to help in preparing me in advance. Even professional people, meaning well and with good intentions, make mistakes in handling parents who lose a child."

The day Sandy went into labor was the day of the first meeting of the SHARE group at St. John's Hospital. There were a couple of mothers who came. One talked to Sandy, and Sandy in turn was able to talk about how she felt. Then the SHARE group started evening sessions so fathers could also attend. Mike and Sandy were able to vent their feelings here. "How unfair it was. It just wasn't right for everyone else to have children. How come we can't have ours? This can't be happening to us." Mike told of the comfort they received at the SHARE meetings. "The doctors never did find out why Sandy went into labor early. The only answers they could come up with were only remote possibilities: that this was a first delivery, that she was thirty-three, and that they were twins. You can go on forever and ask yourself, 'Why?' and you will never get an answer. You can blame other people, and that doesn't work either. But when you can talk to other parents who have been there, it is a tremendous release."

Sandy stayed home for a week and then returned to work. But everyone there treated her as if she had had a disease. "It wasn't out of cruelty. They just didn't know what to say. But that made it harder to bear sometimes than if someone would say something unsympathetic." Although she felt hurt by being avoided, she knew it was good for her to keep busy and work. "In order to get yourself through it, you have to do what is best for you. People have to grieve in the way that helps them, that feels most right for them."

Several days after the death of his sons Mike tried to return to work. After the first day back at his plumbing job a coworker noticed he had total lack of concentration. Then Mike took a fitting and hurled it across the room. He took off the rest of the week to be with Sandy. They did a lot of crying, a lot of talking, and a lot of holding each other. Mike says, "We are blessed in that we have a very open marriage as far as communication is concerned."

Sandy became extremely jealous of Mike's attention to his six-month-old niece, Jennifer. She could not bear the sight of Mike touching Jennifer. She felt he was disloyal to their sons, who had been denied the love he was displaying to Jennifer. When she told Mike about it, Sandy felt ashamed. The possibility of professional help was discussed. At that point the first evening meeting of SHARE was held. Sandy brought up the intense jealousy she felt when Mike was near Jennifer. Mike describes what happened: "As soon as Sandy mentioned her feelings, another mother started to cry. She said that until Sandy spoke, she had thought she was the only one in the world who felt that way. Hearing another mother say this made me more readily able to accept the problem; it made me more understanding of it. Later we learned it was not uncommon."

Mike believes one of the biggest problems bereaved fathers face is not to allow a macho image to be forced on them. "It is infinitely more comforting to hold your wife and cry *with* her. Most women feel that a husband who acts brave doesn't really care the way she does." Mike firmly states fathers should not allow doctors to make all the decisions. "Insist on discussing issues, such as 'Do you want to name the baby? Did you want to have the baby baptized? Do you want to see the baby?'" Mike stresses that if a parent *does* want to see the baby, he or she should insist upon it. He urges parents to take Polaroid pictures. "Otherwise, a parent may be haunted throughout a lifetime by what the baby looked like or a failure to remember features." Mike urges that the wife be included in all the early decisions often brought to the husband to make. "If she is excluded, chances are she will lie in the hospital and wonder about them. She will brood that she was not included in choices about the child, that she was left out and cheated." Mike believes even discussions about flowers and how they might be arranged should be a joint decision between husband and wife.

Mike was able to talk to some of his friends. He came from a big family that was very supportive in the beginning. "But like most of our society, they thought that after a couple of weeks things should be better. They might see you on one particular day when you happened to be down, and they would think you were down all the time. Parents can't stand to see their child hurting, so they try to say things like 'You have to get over this. You're young!'" But Mike says the pain cannot be forced away in this manner. "It's just something you have to work through. It changes your outlook on life. Things that were once important to you are not nearly so important anymore. I don't think it is anything we will ever forget. In time we will be able to live with it, but it does change you. You will never quite be the same person you were."

Mike and Sandy now have one child, two and a half years old. Her name is Candice Marie, and they call her Candi. Sandy is also expecting another child.

"We welcome this opportunity to share with you our experiences with our babies. We are also grateful to you for writing your book because it will be a source of comfort and healing to parents like us." Paula and Matt Fritz shared their experiences in memory of their son, Matthew, and their daughter, Stephanie, both of whom died in 1980. The couple experienced their first loss in January 1979, when Paula miscarried. The pregnancy was ten weeks along. They were disappointed by their loss but accepted it. However, there was an obsession with having a baby, and within three months they were expecting again.

The second pregnancy ended at five months' gestation. The doctors discovered the baby had been miscarried earlier and been undetected. This loss was very difficult for Paula and Matt. They had planned for this baby and were excited about it. "After the doctors told us there was no baby, I remember feeling so empty, so lost. I felt like a freak, being unable to carry a baby. Everyone who is a normal woman can have a baby, I thought. My self-concept and self-confidence took a dive. It hurt me to see my husband hurt, and I felt I was the cause of it all, that my body was my enemy. I was fearful I would never be able to give my husband any babies."

In February 1980, after numerous tests and hormone treatment, Paula became pregnant again. After eight weeks complications began. Her doctors ordered bed rest and hormone injections. At five months' gestation, Paula and Matt discovered they were expecting twins. They were so excited. "Finally, God was going to bless us with children. I began to feel happy again and less like a freak. By seven months along, we were pretty confident that everything would be okay. We had placed our trust in God. We had a specialist as our doctor, and I was being extra-careful. However on August 26, 1980, twins were born ten weeks prematurely. There was no time to help the babies. They both were born with severe hyaline membrane disease. Our son lived six days, and our daughter lived nine days."

Matt and Paula were in shock. "One day we were on cloud

nine, so excited about expecting twins. Then, the next day, we were praying for their lives. The first days after their birth we were on an emotional roller coaster. One minute they were improving; the next they were dying. Our only thoughts were of them. They were in an intensive care unit, and we were able to visit them anytime we wanted." Paula and Matt spent many long hours next to their children, praying for a miracle. Paula remembers touching them, holding them, and just staring at them, trying to memorize their every feature. "Now, sixteen months later, I have trouble remembering all those important details I tried so hard to capture forever."

Paula is grateful to the hospital staff for their kindnesses. "The nurses were so good to us while our babies were in their care. They helped us hold them and touch them. They took lots of pictures of the babies and us. And most important, they gave us choices where our babies were concerned. They told us what our options were regarding such things as holding our babies, visiting with them, and being with them when they were dying. We chose to hold our babies as they were leaving us. We had been with them since conception, and we wanted to share their death with them. The most powerful experience we have ever had was holding our babies as they died. We could sense their love for us as they left us to go to our Father. We could feel God's presence so strongly. It was such a horrifying, yet beautiful experience. As I reflect on those moments, I am filled with a great warmth and renewed closeness to my babies."

After their twins had been buried, family and friends returned to their routines. Paula and Matt were left alone to deal with their grief. "Everyone else forgot our babies and expected us to do the same. At first, we tried forgetting them, but my husband and I could not. It was impossible. We loved them. They were our babies, part of us. They were real and alive. We simply could not forget them. We couldn't find anyone who was comfortable with us talking about our babies. We had no one to turn to who understood. That was when we found the SHARE group."

Paula and Matt needed to talk about their babies. They needed to tell of their experiences and their feelings. "We felt as if we were going crazy at times. We had never before experienced grief. In the other parents who had similar experiences, we found understanding, comfort, and support." After their infants died, the couple felt a flood of emotions—anger, fear, hopelessness, emptiness, loneliness, depression. "Anger, I remember first. We had placed our trust in God, and He had failed us. He took our babies to heaven and left us alone. I felt as if I had lost my best friend, that He had heard my prayers and ignored them. For months I would go to church and just cry. I couldn't even pray anymore. I told God that I was angry at Him, and He would have to wait for me to calm down before I could pray again."

The biggest question for Paula and Matt was—and still is— *why*? At first they tried to think of all the things they might have done to cause God to punish them in this way. They couldn't understand why their babies had had to suffer and die. "We still do not know why, but we have seen a lot of good things happen to us since our babies died." One thing that didn't sit well with the couple was when people told them it was God's will their babies died. "That just increased our anger at God. It was not a consoling statement."

Prior to the loss of their twins, Paula and Matt had been a happy and involved couple. "When our babies died," said Paula, "I actually had times when I felt suicidal. I would never have enough courage to take my life, but many times after their death, I wished I had the gumption. I felt so empty. My life was without hope because I knew I could never have my twins back. I felt so alone. My husband was at my side constantly, giving me all his love and support. He listened endlessly to me talk about our babies and my feelings. He held me close all those long hours I cried. Without his comfort and constant love and sharing of his feelings, I would have thought much more seriously of ending it all."

Life after her son and daughter died was one unending pain for Paula. When she awoke in the morning, her first thought was of Matthew and Stephanie. "Every minute of the day they were not far from my consciousness. Many times, I remember, I wished there was some kind of medicine a person could take to stop the heartache and emptiness." Everyone told Matt and Paula that "time heals all." The hurt is better, but it is still there. "Time has helped us work through the grief process. We have become stronger persons and stronger in our relationship with each other and with God. But whenever we see a preemie baby or talk with parents who have lost children, we feel the pain again—only a little less severely. We will never forget our babies. Through their short, painful lives they gave us so much love, strength, and hope. They are a sign of God's love for us and His Presence in our lives to this very day."

In November 1961 Vivian Kessler and her sister were wheeling their children's carriages. Thanksgiving was approaching, and they were talking about the future—things like how old they were going to be when their children were married. It was a beautiful day, and all was right with their world. This was Vivian's first child. She was twenty-one years old and had been married for a couple of years. She had finished college and was a teacher. Her husband, Joe, worked for a pharmaceutical company. They had bought a house. Life was going along just as planned. Both Vivian and Joe were health-oriented. They applied their knowledge toward eating well and keeping healthy so they would have a beautiful, healthy baby. All their grandparents were still alive. They did all the right things as prospective parents, and Vivian gave birth on time. Robyn weighed seven pounds nine ounces, and her parents were gratified that their conscious application to keeping physically fit had culminated in the birth of a beautiful baby girl.

As Vivian and her sister wheeled the babies, they met a neighbor who invited them to have coffee. The children were sleeping in the carriages outside. Vivian asked her sister to go out and check to make sure Robyn wasn't dressed too warmly. Her sister reported all was okay. After about a half hour visit with their neighbor the two young women returned to the carriages. The sister wheeled her child into her house, and Vivian, who lived just across the street, wheeled Robyn into hers. It was time for lunch, and Vivian heated a bottle for the baby. Vivian picked the infant up but drew back in shock at what she saw. The baby's face was squashed and dark. Vivian screamed her name: "Robyn, Robyn." She thought this must be something that happened to babies and she just didn't know how to handle it because she was a new mother. She ran out to the front of the house and screamed for her sister. When her sister arrived moments later, she took one look and also let out a terrible cry. A neighbor quickly arrived on the scene and took charge. She applied mouth-to-mouth resuscitation and kept doing so in the car en route to the hospital. The nurse at the emergency room grabbed the baby and immediately started to work on her. Vivian was put into a private room. Later someone came in and asked if her husband could be reached, but Vivian never even thought of the word *death*. Moments later, however, she was face-to-face with the word, for the doctor told Vivian her baby could not be saved. Vivian became hysterical. How could her healthy, beautiful child be dead? What did they mean, *dead*? The doctor gave her a hypodermic shot to calm her hysteria. The shot did not numb her but permitted her to realize something would have to be done. She had to go home. Yet she could not go home. She couldn't go back to her house because she knew the carriage would be staring her in the face. No, she could not go home.

At her sister's house she awaited her husband's arrival. As she peered out the window, Vivian saw a woman approach her home across the street. It was a public health nurse who was scheduled for a visit to Robyn. Vivian couldn't look at her. This nurse was coming to see her healthy, beautiful baby— who wasn't healthy, who wasn't beautiful, who was dead! She couldn't talk to her and sent her brother-in-law out to see the nurse. The nurse told him that something like what had happened to Robyn had almost happened to her own daughter. Later a detective arrived to investigate, as in the case of any sudden death. He was kind and gentle, but Vivian clenched her hands when responding to his questions. "Was there a pillow in the crib? What did you feed her for breakfast? What happened during the day?"

Moments later her husband drove up to the house. Vivian couldn't face him. On that particular day he had stopped off to get a haircut and was given a number for his turn. It was something he never did again in future years. He would never take a number at the barber's and always came home first to make sure everything was all right. *Then* he would go and get a haircut. It became one of the ways he found of coping, after two subsequent children.

When her mother-in-law arrived, Vivian blurted out, "I didn't do anything wrong. It wasn't my fault." But deep down inside, thoughts cropped up to haunt her. Had she left the baby in a draft? Had she overdressed her? How could a baby die when she was so well taken care of? What had she done wrong? What troubled Vivian most was that in all the schooling she had had, she never heard that babies could die of "nothing." They waited to hear what the medical examiner said about the death. Her husband called, and the examiner said, "We really don't know. Sometimes babies die, and we just don't know why." Vivian recalls, "He said they had to write something on the death certificate. What appeared were the words *Interstitial pneumonitis.*"

The day after the baby died was a holiday—Thanksgiving— so the funeral was the following day. The funeral home directors had come earlier to Vivian for a dress for Robyn to wear.

Vivian wanted to give them a diaper when suddenly she realized it wasn't needed. Vivian had been haunted by memories of how the baby looked when the child was rushed to the hospital. She asked the funeral directors to allow her to view the body. The baby looked so much better, and it was a lifesaving impression—one Vivian was again and again to superimpose on the terrible scene at the hospital that was implanted in her mind. At home, while people were paying respects and visiting, a roll of film arrived with developed pictures taken earlier of Robyn. Vivian was compelled to show the pictures to her visitors. "This is what my baby looked like." In so doing, she was in effect reinforcing the vision of a beautiful baby over the memory that gave her nightmares for the first two nights. After that week she put the pictures away in a box.

During the first weeks after Robyn's death Vivian and her husband went out to eat a great deal. At home there was nothing to talk about and they played a lot of Scrabble. They hurt too much to talk. There was no gossip. Everything was so trivial. Nothing was important any longer. They abandoned their religion. They felt cheated. Vivian thought: I was a good person. How could babies die? There are so many mean, miserable people, and they are still living. She had seen women who neglected their babies, yet their babies were fine, while she, who had taken such good care of her own well-being prior to the birth, and who had striven to give the best of care to her child, no longer had that child. So how could there be a caring God? She envied the people who could find comfort in religion. But Vivian believed in fairness, and this certainly wasn't fair. "I had been brought up with religion, but it was another of our philosophies that were thrown out. The rituals were nonsensical, and I wanted no part of the trappings."

Vivian found that their way of living changed. While friends were interested in possessions, this was no longer important to Vivian or her husband. But in being angry at the world, they realized they wanted to do something about it. A great deal of their lives was channeled toward a cause—that of the National Sudden Infant Death Syndrome (SIDS) Foundation. Their efforts, along with those of countless others, have done much to enlighten the public that SIDS is *not* caused by suffocation. SIDS is *not* caused by neglect or changing modes of infant care. SIDS *is* a disease that takes the lives of infants without regard to race or socioeconomic status. Eight thousand babies in America will die this year—and no one knows why. The babies—who appear to be normal, healthy infants—will be the victims of Sudden Infant Death Syndrome.

Lydia and Nicholas Volpe, as was the case with so many parents of SIDS babies, knew nothing of this disease. In fact, they didn't really think any baby died in the twentieth century. But their baby did. Their second child, Pamela Lynn, died when she was six weeks old—a full-term, average-birthweight, apparently healthy baby.

Lydia's sister was to be married. In connection with the upcoming nuptials, Lydia accompanied her mother to look for a restaurant for the bridal shower. Pamela was taken by car to be cared for by Lydia's mother-in-law. The baby was put into her carriage, and because it was a balmy day in April, the carriage was placed in the backyard. When Lydia's mother-in-law went to take the baby in to feed her, she noticed the baby was all blue. She quickly called the police, who rushed the baby to the hospital. Nicholas, a systems analyst, was summoned from his job, but Lydia was still out with her mother. As she entered a neighborhood restaurant, Lydia bumped into an uncle who told her she had better go home, that something had happened. She rushed to her mother-in-law's home and found her husband and mother-in-law had returned from the hospital. Pamela was dead. It was unbelievable. Lydia collapsed into a chair after she and Nicholas silently hugged each other. She was numb. What had happened? They must have done something to cause this. Maybe they shouldn't have brought the baby over in the car. Maybe the fumes had caused this to happen. Maybe a cat had come when she was in the yard. What could it be? Pamela was dead on arrival at the hospital. "Yet, when the death certificate came, the cause was listed as acute fulminating broncho-pneumonia. No autopsy was performed."

Sometimes Lydia felt jealous of other people's babies. "I didn't think it was fair. I yearned so for my baby. A priest at church was not supportive. As he did not wish to assume the role of counselor, I got no help. So often the clergy fails a bereaved parent in the early stages of grief. To some parents it may be a comfort to hear 'Your child is an angel' or 'your child is with God.' But others find that upsetting. They want to hear it is all right to be angry for a time and that it is all right to feel as a bereaved parent does—devastated! The clergy should realize they may be the first and sometimes the only person to counsel the bereaved." Lydia went to mass and thought a lot. "How could this terrible thing have happened to us?" She felt if there was no medical explanation, it must have been God's will. "My religious friends would say to me, 'You're very lucky. You have an angel. You will see her in the afterlife.' I wanted her *now*—not in any afterlife! Then I thought of a dear aunt who had died. The thought that perhaps this aunt was with my child did comfort me somewhat."

Lydia began to deal with her grief. The mere smell of baby lotion instantly brought back memories. Pamela died on a Friday, and Lydia remembers thinking Friday must be her bad day. It was also around the time of Lydia's birthday and that of her sister. Now, whenever April rolls around, those occasions are dampened with thoughts of that other sad April day. She recalls giving away some of the baby's clothes to her sister's daughter. "But it was hard seeing them on her child." A year later Lydia was godmother to a little girl. "I was glad to have been asked. It was very traumatic, but I was able to do it. I guess it was a stepping-stone." Every so often the *if onlys* assailed her. If only she hadn't gone out. If only she hadn't put a hat on the baby. If only she hadn't been in the carriage. If only she hadn't given the baby vitamins. If only . . . if only. When they were alone, Lydia kept going over the details with Nicholas. He tried to assure her it wasn't her fault. But was it? What symptom had gone unnoticed? Lydia was to learn later that this guilt is one suffered by every parent whose child has died from SIDS.

Since there was no self-help group at the time of their daughter's death, family friends and a physician were called upon for support. "One knows and remembers well those who were supportive. One does not forget the comments that were destructive. Both the informed and the uninformed take pot-luck guesses as to what they think you did or did not do to contribute to this death. 'Was the baby on her stomach?' Or 'It must have been the anesthesia you had at the time of delivery.' Those who find themselves in the position of the 'supporters' would do best to listen and listen hard, offering no simple solutions."

With their two subsequent children, Lydia and Nicholas made valiant attempts to watch them when they slept but soon found this too wearing and eventually gave up. Nicholas became the one who checked the babies throughout the night. "Though our subsequent children were anxiously awaited, they did not replace Pamela. Slowly the *if onlys* faded, and self-confidence returned. Each wondrous day they are alive bears witness to the fact that it must not have been our fault." Their pediatrician became a patient and trusted friend. At the time of their baby's death Lydia and Nicholas rushed their first child in for a checkup. They were afraid the same mysterious illness would possibly claim their son's life. "We flooded the doctor with phone calls and inquiries in the hope he could forestall another disaster. He was most understanding and supportive. Later he joined the medical board of our chapter of the NSIDSF and today is still helping parents whose babies have died or whose babies have periodic apnea [an episode of non-breathing during sleep] and may need monitors."

Lydia states their "supportive" relatives and friends were encouraging and optimistic. "They understood my very sad moments, hours, and days. They did not tell me to forget about it or that it was 'only a baby. You'll have another.' Pamela died in 1961. Since there were several years before the inception of what is now the National Sudden Infant Death Syndrome Foundation, I needed these understanding people. Once I became involved in the work of the Foundation, it was comforting to be in the company of other couples who had suffered as we did. It was comforting to begin helping others. I founded a chapter in the New York City area, trained the NYC public health nurses, instituted parent meetings, lectured on SIDS, and helped with necessary fund raising. To this day I am available to parents who need to talk to someone else whose baby died and who has recovered."

At times Lydia is asked, "Where are you today, these many years after your baby's death?" As chairperson of the Community Advisory Council of the New York City Information and Counseling Program for SIDS, Lydia sometimes wonders what people think of her involvement, although it is so many years past. "I still think about that time of my life. It hurts a little most days of the week. There are so many reminders, but mostly it is within me. I had four children, and now I have three. One died. Even though death is a private matter, I want to share it if in some way other parents can gain strength. That is why I am still here."

5 · Husbands and Wives

- "A month after our son died, my husband asked for a divorce. That was the icing on the cake."
- "When we were told our daughter was killed, my husband became a raving lunatic. He had to talk, talk, talk constantly. There was never a moment of peace when I could cry alone."
- "My wife cried all the time. I couldn't bear to look at her after a while. I had to get out of the house, anywhere."
- "I knew my husband blamed me for our daughter's death. We could not sit down at the breakfast table any longer. We could not look at each other without my feeling the guilt."
- "The first answer my husband had to the problem was having sex. To him, he needed it. It was a release. To me, it was unthinkable."
- "We seem to spend most of our time yelling at each other, and what we say hurts. It's as if the yelling and screaming were a kind of 'painfest' of letting out what we can't say to others."
- "I know he is seeing someone else. He doesn't come home until late. He doesn't eat here. We can't talk. He doesn't want to even let me speak our son's name."
- "There were constant arguments over money. My wife began to drink heavily. The cost of our daughter's illness had drained us. And I resented her adding to our burden."

In order to protect their surviving children and to maintain confidentiality, the names of the parents in this chapter are not given. And because some spouses may find ways to communicate or reconcile, that anonymity is offered to them. Some parents have survived as couples and are able to continue life together on a very high level. Others have separated. Many couples have divorced. Still others have remarried.

Each person is so different, so individual, there is no specific list of do's or don'ts that can apply. As one parent succinctly put it, "There are no rights, and there are no wrongs. Yet, there are right things to do and wrong things to do. The whole thing is a contradiction. Losing a child is a contradiction." Although couples don't have to fall into certain stages of grief, each person falls into them with only the time frame being different. Each person has his or her own calendar when it comes to grieving. Sometimes there is shock. In some people there is resignation. In others there is total despondency. Often in grief, couples feel they have to act in a particular way because it is *expected* of them. This outrages many parents. One spouse said, "Many couples behave in a way they feel they should for the benefit of other people. This cuts into the ways husbands and wives could begin to start breaking out of their grief patterns. Parents worry so about things like 'What would my mother say if . . .' or 'What will the children think if . . .' One family slept with the bedroom door open so their teenage children wouldn't think they were involved in sex. People are brainwashed because no one has told them *how* to do things or that it is all right to do them."

One couple told of the first time they went out and of a later vacation. They were looking for some sort of relief from the unrelenting pain they felt. Wondering what others would think of their actions, they found a way to avoid running into anyone. "We had to get out. We had to feel like human beings again, even if for a minute. But then came the syndrome: 'What are people going to think if you are seen laughing, or if they see you at a restaurant, smiling, eating, talking?' They expect to see these morose people whose child is dead. When we went out for the first time, we went to an area where we weren't known. We went out privately. We took a walk on the beach hand in hand. We talked about our son, and we cried a little. Later we went to dinner at a place we had never been before, where our friends normally wouldn't go. Then we went to Hawaii—a very faraway place so that we could do and think as two people on vacation. We were not the bereaved parents. When we came back, we had seen movies. We had laughed. We had eaten. We had joked. And of course, we had cried. But we had done things, positive things. So by the time we came back we were over that hump of people seeing us do things."

As for sex and the marriage, most people don't want to talk about this touchy subject. Different people require sex in different ways. Some people, when they are under a lot of stress, couldn't think of sex in a million years. Other people, when they are involved in a stressful situation, whether it be bankruptcy or illness in the family or anything, turn to sex. This is an outlet for them. Some women become very cold because they find the very thought of sex, or any connotation of pleasure, abhorrent. Too, the husband represents the procreator of the dead child. Memories of sex that culminated in the birth of their child often cannot be reconciled with the idea of sex after the death of their child. Many wives cannot fathom how their husbands can be thinking of sex at a time like this. "How can my husband want sex when our child is just dead a week? He is just an animal with no thought for my grief." Conversely, there are also husbands who turn away because of the aggressive woman: "How can she possibly want sexual enjoyment now? She is insatiable, but at a time like this? How can she expect it?"

One wife told of her feelings when her husband asked her to resume sexual intercourse. "I was horrified. I felt he was totally insensitive and uncaring that he could even suggest it. I know my refusal brought problems, and later I know he started seeing other women. But there was no way I could comply. We could not communicate on any level. He refused to talk about our son. He wanted only to plaster the walls with his pictures. Everywhere you turned, you saw my son. I couldn't take it. And I left—with only *one* picture of my son. I took with me only the last picture ever taken of him." In other instances fathers who have lost a child are often unable to express grief openly—to either their mates or those closest to them. In many instances sex represents a release from the pain of grief, albeit brief. Enjoyment of sex can help diminish pain, and that has to be a plus. Any relief from anguish is desirable.

Then there are the most healthy of couples who have within the first week turned to each other. One such husband and wife told of their first return to having sex after the death of their child. "It did not start out as 'Hey, you want to have a roll in the hay?' It started as two people who turned to each other, sobbing and crying in bed, holding each other because they were grieving over the loss of their child. And from that holding and that warmth and that closeness came the sexual relationship. In a good marriage, sex is not just for the physical 'Hey, that feels good, let's do it.' Sex is an all-encompassing sharing of love. It is touching and caring, and a very beautiful thing. And what better time than when you are in pain and needing help should this beautiful thing take place?"

There are people who have had problems dealing with sex in the first place. "Some feel sex is 'dirty' or have feelings of 'do it with the light out.' For those who have been taught that sex is a no-no to begin with, how can you expect them to do something others consider enjoyable when they feel it's something you are not supposed to do anyway?" In other instances, mates react when spouses hide behind sex to justify their grief. One spouse described this: "I know a couple of men who have turned to having affairs because their wives had turned so completely cold. One of the women now feels perfectly justified in being frigid because 'After all, look what I have gone through!' One of the first things that helps somebody get over the terrible suffering that *you* have gone through is to know 'Hey, lady, you are not alone, a lot of other people have gone through this; you want to die, but you can't. The pain is really unbearable, but you're not the only person who ever endured it.' "

There are stresses also in marriage because we all know each

other's weaknesses. And after a child dies, a parent is extremely vulnerable. One can either work on those weaknesses or
push them aside and work on strengths. After a child has died,
there is an underlying need to find out the *why?* Because no
satisfactory answer is found, a parent often directs this anger
toward the spouse. This is how a parent uses grief in the most
negative way. In many instances anger on the part of one parent and guilt on the part of the other are a street with a dead
end—with no way to vault the brick wall facing them.

The circumstances of a child's death create many of the
problems. For example, one young boy had a habit of leaving
his lunch box at school. His mother told her son when he left
for school in the morning not to forget it. The husband ad-
monished the wife for always "pestering" the child about it.
The boy *did* forget it and told his school chums he had to go
back and get the lunch box. When he did, he was killed on his
bicycle by an oncoming truck. The father vented his anger as
to the *why?* against his wife. He claimed if she had not pressed
their son about always remembering the lunch box, he
wouldn't have been distracted, wouldn't have gone back, and
the child would still be alive.

Too, unless spouses agree upon the course of treatment
when a child has a terminal illness, tremendous hostility can
result. One parent may wish to continue radiation, while the
other may wish to call halt and cease. One mate may wish to
leave the child in the hospital, while the other may want to
bring the child home. One husband and wife, whose four-year-
old daughter was dying of an incurable disease, told of some of
the pressures: "In the early stages of her illness our initial feelings were never to have another baby. The guilt we felt for the
birth of our little girl who was now suffering so terribly was
too much to bear." However, as the disease progressed, it became an obsession to the couple to have another child before
they gave this one up. The two parents agreed on this issue, as
they did on all the important ones, such as the hospitalization,
whether to keep their child home or not, etc. "Every time an

important decision had to be made we were together on it. We were friends to begin with, a very important prerequisite, because if external pressures are so great, then disagreement can wreck the marriage."

In attempts to understand the high ratio of separation and divorce among couples after the loss of a child, the Association for Marriage and Family Therapy was contacted. Dr. Ruth Neubauer, president of the New York chapter, comments on this high incidence: "Sorrow and grief can also bring people closer together. It is my feeling some marriages that fail after the death of a child may not have been good marriages to begin with and may have failed for other reasons. Those couples may have been more parents than marriage partners. They may have done a lot of blaming the other rather than take responsibility for their own part in a problem. Losing a child often puts marriage to a severe test, and it is wise for such couples to seek individual and marital help."

After the death of their daughter one husband began to react to his wife's drinking. "Before our daughter died, my wife was just a social drinker. She never drank to excess. In fact, I never saw her drunk. But we had monetary problems. Every time we turned around there were more bills: doctors' bills; hospital bills—a seemingly unending expenditure of money. Although I made a good salary, there just was never enough to cover all the expenses. My wife's answer to this was to drink, drink, drink. I guess she just couldn't face it. I would call from work in the early afternoon, and I would hear that her speech was already slurring. When I came home at night, she was reeling. There was never any supper ready. There was never any show of affection, just drunken weeping. She drove me crazy." The husband relates he could not put up with this any longer after one year. He decided on a divorce. A trial separation was suggested by his lawyer. The husband had his doubts but agreed to give it a chance. One year later there was an attempt at a reconciliation. However, his wife would go on drunken binges. "I tried very hard. I really didn't want to end my marriage, and I thought I would give it another try, to see if she could snap out of it and get rid of the drinking somehow. But her behavior left me no choice. I knew if I didn't get out, I would drown."

In another instance a wife became intensely religious after the death of her son. Before the child's death she had gone to church only occasionally. Now all this changed. The wife felt their son's death was partially due to the family's lack of strong religious faith. This was a penance now to be paid—by everyone in the family. Her husband balked. "I just wasn't able to accept that God punished us in this way. I can't believe God would take away our child because we didn't go to church." Religion was not the answer to his grief, but he bowed to his wife's wishes where their surviving children were concerned.

It is not only the parents who suffer in relationships with their spouses. After the death of her brother a surviving daughter tells of the strain placed on her marriage. It was very difficult for her husband to relate to her loss or that felt by her parents. She had been married only a short time. "I am not the same person I was. It is hard for my husband to accept this new person. I am not the person he married. He feels cheated because I spend so much time with my parents. He feels that my parents come first and he comes second." There is a lot of bitterness in the marriage. "I feel this is my time to grieve, and I don't feel I have to be the peacemaker in all this. I feel a lot of resentment for some of the cold things he has said to me and the lack of a shoulder to cry on. He was there for the first three months just like everyone else I knew. After a period of time, say, two or three months, everyone thinks you should be okay. That was the time when I really needed him to be there. And that is when he wasn't there."

Another surviving daughter had similar problems with her mate. Her husband was resentful of her actions. He was annoyed that she continued to visit the cemetery. He was angry that she wanted to buy a new dress for her sister to be buried in and irritated at other expenditures he felt her parents should have borne. The daughter was expressing love and wasn't concerned with the monetary angles her husband was criticizing. "I wanted to do something for my sister. I loved her, and I wanted to buy her dress. It wouldn't dawn on me to ask my parents to pay for a dress I had given as a token of love." She felt that her husband was unduly critical of money at her time of grief.

One bereaved parent summed it up this way: "Prior to marriage, during the courtship period, everything comes up roses. After all, you are in love. And love conquers all. Faults are of no consequence in the face of romance. When two people marry, they begin the facing of issues and the acceptance that these same faults make up everyday living, just as their love for their spouse does. But throughout a marriage, faults or no, there is generally a support network of some substance. After the death of their child that support network may be shattered. A lot of couples can suffer from disillusionment when each expects too much from the other. They have to maintain an open line of communication, and if one doesn't want to talk and the other does, they have to reach a détente like Russia and America. There has to be a specific time set aside to talk if that is the case. A lot of times couples can't really express their true emotions to each other, and after the loss of a child this is even harder. A lot of times either the husband or the wife may try to conform to what other people think, how others believe they should act, instead of how they *really* want to act. This business of trying to be sure to please other people can get to be a real hang-up in marriages. But the main thing is to remember that you brought a child into the world together. You shared a bed together. You agreed to a marriage for better or for worse. The worst that there could ever be is to lose your child. No marriage should ever have to be put to that test. But when it is, the two people involved shouldn't kill each other. They should fight the world together."

6 · Surviving Brothers and Sisters

Lee Irish died at the age of thirteen while traveling with his family through Europe. In Rome the boy contracted acute meningitis, which claimed his life. Lee's brother, Jeff, wrote a poem a few days after his older brother's death. Typed on a borrowed typewriter, Jeff's tribute is reproduced below in its original form.

A BOY THIRTEEN

He had red hair,
Was thin and tall,
One could never eat as much as he,
He hiked in the sierras,
Went back-packing and even planned
a trip for the family,
Even got me to join Boy Scouts,
Always wanted me to backpack with him,
We went to Germany,
He and I to German schools and learned German,
      went
Then it came time for our trip to Rome,
By train,
He and I couldnt wait to come back to
Germany and go sledding,
We passed through the Alps on the way
to Rome,
I looked up to him,
I twelve and HE "A BOY THIRTEEN",
He was five feet and nine inches tall,
I remember very well looking up and there
HE was with the train window down, His head
a little ways out §§§ § with the wind blowing

§ § his red hair as he watched the Alps
passing by,
He was my brother,
my only § brother,

———

One I could play Baseball with,
Someone I could talk to,
In Germany he had bought a camera,
A single lense reflex,
HE had alot of new things going on,
Then on Feb. 6 He died.
He my only brother the one I planned to
backpack with, the guy I wanted to sled with,
the person I looked up to, the boy that
played baseball with me, the guy with a
new camera, my brother who I could talk to, the
one who could eat as no one else, my brother that
was five feet and nine inches tall, tall and thin with
red hair "THE BOY THAT WAS THIRTEEN":
He died because he happened to breath in some bacteria
that probably can only be seen under some special microscope,
I guess all I can say is §§§§ I loved him and needed him and
that I dont understand.

A great fear of surviving children is that of being left alone.
This frightening thought is not an uncommon reaction. Children suffer the terror that their parents or other siblings might also die and leave them. The surviving child often wonders if he will suffer the same fate as befell his sibling. Although children may appear to be functioning well again, these fears and anxieties can remain throughout a lifetime if left unrelieved. The best way to rid the child's mind of such frightening thoughts is for parents, friends, and family members to express as often as possible their reassurance to the child. Explain that what happened to his sibling occurred for a specific reason and it will not happen to him, to his parents, or to his other sisters and brothers.

It is important that a child not confuse death with sleeping. One young boy was fearful of going to bed because he was told his sister had died in her sleep. Death should be explained in a simple manner. A child should be told in ways he can comprehend that being dead and going to sleep are not the same. If these fears are not dispelled, the child may develop a fear of sleeping, thinking that if God took one child while sleeping, then God can come and take him as well.

Guilt is a reaction common to children upon the death of a sibling. The surviving child needs to be able to free himself or herself of guilt feelings, but often cannot. Author Harold Sherman tells of the terrible guilt he suffered when his younger brother, Edward, died at the age of eleven. On a beautiful October day Harold, then a boy of sixteen, was preparing to bicycle back to his high school when a premonition overtook him. In his book *How to Know What to Believe,* Harold tells what happened on that fateful day:

> I saw that my younger brother, Edward, age eleven, had climbed the tree in our front yard, between the sidewalk and the street, and I had a fleeting vision of his falling and getting seriously hurt.
>
> My impulse at the moment was to stop and call him down and make him promise not to climb that tree again. I reached in my pocket and took out a nickel with the thought that if I offered this to him, it would be an added inducement for him to keep such a promise, although Edward was such a truthful little fellow, I knew whatever he promised would be done.
>
> But a nickel meant more to a boy in those days than it does now. I juggled the coin in my hand and decided I was worrying about something that wouldn't happen; so I shoved it back in my pocket and dismissed my feeling of apprehension as I rode off to school, waving Edward good-bye.

Several hours later, returning home from school, Harold heard cries of excruciating pain and arrived to see neighbors carrying Edward into the Sherman house. Harold's young brother had come home from his nearby grade school and had climbed the tree again. Only this time a rotten limb had broken off, and Edward had been catapulted onto the concrete ground. The fall was so severe that both arms were badly broken, with bones coming through the flesh. The boys' parents were out on a boat ride with a cousin, and only a live-in maid, Margaret, was present at the time of the accident. Edward was brought to his parents' bedroom downstairs. His pitifully broken arms were placed on pillows.

The family physician arrived and asked that the dining room table be cleared. Edward was carried gently and laid upon it. The doctor then applied chloroform to the boy and began the tedious work of setting the fractures. Harold was called upon to assist, holding his brother's body securely and giving the doctor whatever instruments he called for. All this time Harold was plagued by the thought that none of this would have happened if he had given Edward that nickel and had made him promise not to climb the tree. If only he had . . . if . . . if . . .

Harold was tormented by the guilt feelings that assailed him after having been warned of the impending tragedy by his premonition. He agonized that he had had an opportunity to prevent the accident and felt somehow he had failed. How could he ever forgive himself? He wondered if that nickel could have possibly been more important to him than his brother's life. He tried to comprehend why he had talked himself out of extracting a promise from Edward. Why hadn't he paid attention to the premonition? Now it was too late. Now Harold's young brother had two broken arms, crudely set. The doctor had found it extremely difficult to place the protruding bones back into their position with the facilities available.

As soon as his brother was returned to bed, Harold jumped on his bicycle and quickly rode to the bayfront where his cousin's boat was kept. He raced out onto the dock, scanning the waters for a glimpse of the boat, but there was no sign of it. He was frantic with the thought that his parents were somewhere out on the water, completely unknowing of the terrible accident that had befallen his brother.

> Why did this have to happen? If there was an all-merciful, all-loving God, as I had been taught, how could He have permitted my innocent little brother, who had brought such joy and brightness to all those his life had touched, to suffer such an injury?
>
> Up to this time, I had not been confronted with such questions. But now it was all so frighteningly impersonal; the world suddenly seemed so cold and cruel and unfeeling, and God so very far away.

Harold desperately awaited his parents' return. When they arrived, his father told Harold he had had a foreboding that something was wrong at home. Both parents were instantly faced by another question: If they had been home, would the accident have happened? Would Edward have found other activities to occupy himself rather than climb the tree?

Tragically, after forty-eight hours, tetanus infection developed. On the sixth day Edward seemed to sense that he was about to depart this life, and he called each member of the family to him, puckered his lips, and kissed them good-bye, one by one.

At the funeral the minister said, "We can't understand why such a tragedy should befall one of God's children. Many who knew Edward Sherman have said that he was too good for this life and that they were sure God, in His wisdom, had needed him in Heaven and had called him home." These comments created great inner turmoil in Harold, and a furious rebellion arose within him:

> I thought if God had had anything to do with my brother falling from a tree, suffering those injuries and almost unbearable pain, only to die—cutting short such a promising young life— then He was not the kind of God I could worship. He was more

a sadistic fiend than a loving Father, and I would damn such an idea of God the rest of my life if I was to burn in hell for it!

I was tortured enough by the thoughts that I had been given a foreknowledge of this happening and had done nothing about it. This might well plague me the rest of my life. Had my brother's life depended upon my heeding this warning? Why did so many things occur that seemingly could have been prevented if someone had said or done something differently? Perhaps in the lives of all people, there have been deeds and misdeeds for which they have suffered deep regret and remorse and which, once committed, could not be recalled or atoned. This hardly made the bearing any easier.

In Edward's case, he had climbed the tree of his own free will, had reached up and gotten hold of a rotten limb, which had broken under the stress and strain, leading to his fall. It was now clear to me that there is Cause and Effect behind everything that happens, however small and seemingly insignificant. No thing happens by chance. Our unthinkably great Creator has established laws for all life to follow. Obedience or disobedience to these laws, however knowingly, willfully, or blindly, determines whether or not they operate for or against us.

It is a mistake to blame our concept of God for things that go wrong. We must assume our share of responsibility for whatever happens, much of which we bring upon ourselves, directly or indirectly.

This realization helped me to accept what had happened on a human level, without involving God.

In attempting to understand what had permitted him to foresee his brother's accident, Harold Sherman has spent a lifetime of research in the field of extrasensory perception. He established the ESP Research Associates Foundation for exploration of the origin and nature of man's sixth sense. Seeking answers to why he had sensed the accident in advance, Harold embarked upon a crusade to cast light on dependable psychic and spiritual knowledge. To that end, he has written innumerable self-help books on the subject, most of them best sellers.

Madeleine Toomey also experienced anger at God when her sister, Kathleen, age twenty-three, was killed in a car accident caused by a drunken driver. Madeleine kept asking, "Why? Why?" She felt God had let her down and stopped going to church. Madeleine first learned of her sister's death when she received a telephone call from her mother early one morning. Upon hearing the news, she began to scream. Her husband had already left for work, and her ten-year-old son, Erik, was awakened by her shouting. After ten minutes she attempted to compose herself to calm her young son and to explain to him that his aunt Kathy had died in a car crash.

At the funeral home the family was plagued by local reporters and photographers who wanted to ask questions and take pictures of her parents. The directors of the funeral parlor had to be summoned to remove the newspeople, who were turning the service into a circus. Madeleine was bitter and angry at the insensitivity of the reporters to the family's loss. Later she was also angry at her friends who were squeamish about listening to her express her grief. She understands, and forgives them, but was lost by having no real friend to hear her anguished thoughts. For the first six months she went to the cemetery twice a day and, together with her surviving sisters, bought cemetery plots next to Kathleen's grave. Madeleine's grief took many forms. At work there were glass tubes nearby. Her first week back at work she sat and cried the whole time. Suddenly, upon seeing the glass tubes, she wanted to smash them. Instead, she vented this anger in other ways. Sometime back, she had joined a soccer team. Later she was able to get a lot of frustration and anger out of her system by participating in the sport. Only now is she able to sleep through the night. For months she kept dreaming about the telephone call from her mother telling her of Kathleen's death. Madeleine kept trying to redream that call, trying to produce a dream in which the accident never happened.

Madeleine and her surviving sisters and brothers were saddened by their parents' comments: "Why couldn't it have been me instead? We have lived our life." She had never seen her father cry. "To see my father in that state made me feel it was me suffering so badly rather than him, and I would hurt even more inside." Madeleine doesn't recall the first week after her sister's death. "I don't remember who told me to breathe or comb my hair." She later had chest pains, palpitations, and difficulty in sleeping and was given a mild tranquilizer to calm her. Her ability to function was impaired on many levels for months to come. It was to be more than six months before Madeleine was able to add even a simple column of figures because her concentration was so interrupted. She could not write a bank check or do any type of simple calculation properly during that time.

The first two months after her sister's death, Madeleine skipped her menstrual cycle. She panicked, thinking she couldn't possibly be pregnant, but something was wrong. She visited her gynecologist, who assured her she was fine, not pregnant, that stress was the culprit creating the change in her cycle. A few weeks after Kathleen died, Madeleine also broke out in acne, something she had never had before. Her dermatologist linked it with the same emotional upheaval, and it was cleared up with antibiotic medication.

Kathleen's death had occurred a few weeks before Easter. And somehow Madeleine thought something wonderful would happen on that forthcoming day. "In church I kept hearing the story of Lazarus, and in the back of my mind I kept hoping Kathleen would raise from the dead on Easter Sunday. I really had such hope that when Easter came, I was terribly disappointed." During the Christmas season Madeleine received many Christmas cards, some of which were from friends who had never got in touch with her when her sister died. This lack of communication from friends was also a great disappointment to Madeleine.

One of the things Madeleine found most difficult was telling people her sister had died. "When someone who did not know my sister would come to our home and would see the pictures up all over the house, the inevitable questions would come: 'Who is the girl in the pictures?' It's very hard." Yet Madeleine wants the pictures to stay in view. For with them, there is something of Kathleen remaining, too.

In a positive effort to be of assistance to others, Madeleine became involved in the efforts of the organization called RID—Remove Intoxicated Drivers, helping to push legislation and working toward helpful goals.

As in Madeleine's case, it is not uncommon to see physical illness beset parents of a child who has died. At the top of the list are complaints of arthritis, loss of appetite, headaches, insomnia, heart palpitations, ulcerated colitis, muscular aches, pains, and minor accidents. Surviving brothers and sisters suffer similar ailments. Dr. Leonard Stieglitz was one such surviving sibling. His brother died of Hodgkin's disease at the age of twenty-one. A young dentist, Dr. Stieglitz suddenly found he could no longer perform in his office. He could not even remember basic early work learned in dental school. After developing ulcerated colitis, he sought psychiatric assistance to help him conquer the severe depression and deep anxieties brought on by his brother's illness. His four-year-old daughter seemed able to accept the loss of her uncle, but she suffered traumatic effects two years later when her grandmother died. Dr. Stieglitz recalls, "She was very disruptive in school and would cry a great deal. It was only through the understanding nature of a sympathetic teacher that my daughter was allowed to remain at school rather than be sent home to us." The child was frightened of going to school and leaving her parents because she was afraid they would not be there when she came home. With the cooperation of the teacher, Dr. Stieglitz and his wife were able to allay the child's fears.

Stephanie Allen recalls she felt she shouldn't cry at her brother's funeral. There were more than a thousand people there, and Stephanie worked so hard to keep it all inside that she could never break through that wall again. At the funeral she felt that if she cried, she would be exposing part of herself to all those people. "For the first twenty-four hours, whatever my defense mechanisms were, they put me into a place where I didn't feel anything." After her brother's death Stephanie went to a psychiatrist. "He told me I must feel guilty, that he had felt responsible for his mother's death." Stephanie had been living away from home at the time of her brother's death. "I had no pangs of guilt but felt as if I were listening to the psychiatrist's problem about his mother." She later saw another psychiatrist. "The doctor kept telling me how wonderful I was. And I would ask, 'Then how come I feel like shit?'" Stephanie remained in therapy for a couple of months and then was able to move forward on her own, making decisions about moving, relocating.

The outstanding thing Stephanie remembers as being extremely painful to her was that she was left as the only surviving child. "I hated holidays and feeling like an only child. I wanted to be part of a big family with lots of kids, and I certainly did not want to be an only child." Stephanie's parents ultimately divorced, causing her great inner turmoil. "It took away my history. It wasn't a friendly divorce. There was no way to reminisce as a family. I didn't have my brother to reminisce with, and then there was no family to do this with. My mother has a new husband; my father has a new family. The one thing is that I have known my mother's husband since I was a kid, and that's nice for me." Stephanie believes it is very important for people to sit down and really to talk—to express their emotions and let their feelings be known. "People have a tendency to say, 'Don't talk about it.' But solutions can be arrived at only when people communicate."

On the morning of June 9, 1981, Jay Goldstein heard the alarm ring. It had been set to waken his brother Philip, who had a paper route to deliver mornings. Because Philip didn't hear the alarm, Jay told his brother it was time to get up. That action—alerting his brother that the alarm had gone off—was to bother Jay one day later. Because one day later his brother was dead. Philip died on June 10, 1981, having been hit by a car the previous morning while delivering newspapers on his bike.

Jay and Philip shared a bedroom. Had Jay *not* shared his brother's room and *not* heard the alarm, he couldn't have told his brother about it. Then somehow maybe the accident would have been avoided, Jay thought. Too, until three months earlier, Jay also had a paper route. He and Philip used to go off to work together in the mornings. Somehow, Jay reasoned, if he had still had that paper route and had left with Philip, this wouldn't have happened.

Today Jay realizes that nothing he did or did not do caused the accident. But guilt feelings created much inner turmoil in the early months of his grief. Jay urges other siblings not to let the burdens of guilt and grief encompass you. "It's better to talk about your feelings and to get them out of your system. You learn that others feel the same as you do."

Jay had been concerned about a dream he had the morning of Philip's accident. He dreamed he heard ambulance sirens and his brother was carried away on a stretcher in an ambulance. After talking about the dream, Jay was not frightened of it. He came to understand that in life we sometimes experience things that perhaps buffer the impact of a shock by learning of them through psychic impressions.

Jay was able to convey some of his feelings in a talk given by him at Smithtown High School West. There Mrs. Barbara Okst teaches a course entitled "Death: A Fact of Life." There is a waiting list of students who want to take the course. Why?

Because Mrs. Okst, an innovative and caring teacher, has brought in dynamic speakers who present views on death from many standpoints, allowing ample opportunity for questions by the class. One such speaker was Angela Purpura, chairperson of the Long Island, New York, chapter of The Compassionate Friends. Representing that organization's siblings group, Jay accompanied Angela to speak to the class. He was able to explain to his fellow teenagers how he felt when his brother died, of his guilt feelings and how he was attempting to cope. "I wasn't really able to talk to my parents or anyone else, but at The Compassionate Friends' siblings' group, I could open up and talk because I knew the others there would understand." Jay told of hearing a teenager talking about paraplegics. "She said, 'I would die if anyone in my family was a paraplegic.' I kept my feelings in, but I was thinking: 'I would rather have a person alive than dead.' "

Jay, now fifteen, has a younger brother, Joshua, who is nine. Joshua also had problems after his brother's death. He learned that everyone grieves in different ways and you have to do what is most comfortable for you. Joshua has also learned other children feel much the same as he does—that they have similar fears and similar ways of grieving. At first Joshua had difficulty sleeping at night if his parents were out. He would wait for them to come home. He was frightened they might not, that maybe something would happen to them as had happened to Philip. Later Joshua began to understand that what happened to Philip did not mean it would happen to him or his parents. But fears are natural in all of us, and Joshua's fears were not unusual. He is a brave boy to come forward and share his inner thoughts so other children won't be afraid they are experiencing something no one else ever has.

Joshua was in class when Philip died. A call came through on the intercom system to his teacher, asking that Joshua report to the principal's office. "When I went in, the principal told me Philip had died. He said if Philip had lived, he would have been a vegetable." In his child's mind, Joshua could not conceive of what his brother would have looked like as a vegetable. Many adults, unable to speak at a child's level, can do a great deal of harm unintentionally. "I guess maybe he didn't want me to feel bad." But Joshua did feel bad. Very bad indeed. He missed playing with his older brother, who used to beat him up—ever so lovingly. He remembers when Philip would play the trumpet and how he liked to play soccer.

It was close to the end of school semester when Philip died. The following September Joshua returned to school. He brought with him a newspaper article about Philip's death. When he started to read it to the class, he began to cry. The teacher finished reading the story. Joshua has learned it is all right to cry when you are unhappy. And it is all right to remember your brother. After all, he did exist, and there are memories we all want to keep.

Eloise Shields, a mother who teaches in the Torrance school district in California, understands that young children need help in their grief: "Many teachers have come to me, asking for emotional support for and information about children who are experiencing grief and loss in their classrooms. Often a child will come to school and pour out his soul to a teacher, and she doesn't know how to handle it. Generally teachers are so busy that they don't try to take on too much therapy with a child. But just listening is often all that is needed if the emotion isn't too strong in the child." However, if the child experiences deeper grief, the parent is asked to come in to get more facts, and the teacher can see if the parent is aware of what the child is going through.

"One explicit direction is given to the parent, to *make* the child come to school, whether he wants to or not. It is not uncommon for a child to want to stay home if he has lost a sister, brother, or parent. The loss is so overwhelming he doesn't want to leave home, just in case someone else leaves him forever. So he dreams up the reasoning that if he never leaves home, he'll always be around to prevent anyone else from leaving him unexpectedly. Parents have to be shored up to remain firm, that life is to go on at school as usual. This alone is a great help to both parent and child, for the school to tell them this rule. We've found this prevents the child from developing a school phobia, which is much harder to treat than the death adjustment, for it compounds the emotional adjustment."

A further aid for parents in helping their children deal with the death of a family member is available free from: National Institute of Mental Health, 5600 Fishers Lane, Rockville, MD 20857. The title of the pamphlet is "Caring About Children: Talking to Children About Death."

Many misconceptions arise in a child's mind after the death of a sibling. Dr. Roberta Temes, clinical assistant professor, Department of Psychiatry, Downstate Medical School, Brooklyn, New York, and author of *Living with an Empty Chair,* offers some suggestions in understanding the needs of surviving children:

> Children need to talk in order to clarify. They must be told that the person is dead. Other "stories" do not work. The child must be told that death is final. When parents do not use the term "dead" they encourage hope.
>
> If you plan to explain the concept of heaven to a child you must carefully choose your words. Children calmly take things literally. Stewardesses report that each plane to Disneyland has at least one child peering out the window trying to locate the grandma who died. Children have been known to ask, "If brother went to heaven, why are you burying him in the earth?" One young child thought that bodies were "planted" in the ground so that new ones would grow.
>
> The grief of a child for a parent or sibling is particularly painful. To a child, death may be taken as the ultimate rejection. In childish magical thinking, death occurs because of a deed or a wish. Some children, convinced that they caused the death, feel guilty for the remainder of their lives.

While most adults begin the first stage of mourning immediately, children usually begin mourning several weeks or months after the death. Children should not be criticized for caring, selfishly, about their own personal needs. . . . They sometimes postpone mourning until they are assured that all their needs for survival will be taken care of. Once they are positive that their physical and psychological security will not be snatched from them, they will relax and feel, and weep, and begin the mourning process.

Children may need to be shown evidence that illness does not necessarily lead to death. We all get sick and we all recover; health is a natural state. It is the rare exception who succumbs to disease.

Cara Purpura, now eight, was almost six years old when her sister, Cassandra, died. Cassandra's best friend, Eileen, then became a good friend to Cara. Cara feels extremely close to Eileen. "When I am with Eileen, I feel like I am with half of Cassandra." Although Cara has found joy in her friendship with Eileen, she has had problems with other children. One school chum came to stay overnight at Cara's house. However, before the night was out, the young visitor cried hysterically and asked to go home. Later Cara told her mother her friend had been afraid that Cassandra's ghost would come in the night.

Cara also had to face the ghoulish humor of other children. "One boy kept asking me, 'How is your sister?' even though he knew she was dead." Another sensitive issue Cara had to deal with was one encountered by many a younger sister or brother in school. Often when a teacher has more than one child from the same family, the teacher reverts to calling the child by the name of the sibling taught earlier. When Cara's teacher slipped and called her Cassandra, it was extremely offensive to Cara. She refused to respond. Cara brought the issue to a head and pointed out the error to the teacher. Cara is a survivor, and will not be identified as anyone other than Cara. And if her teacher expected her to pay attention and learn, then she could fully expect the same of her teacher.

Once, when Cara visited her friend Eileen's home, some photographs were being shown. Among them was a picture of Cara and Cassandra in an early pose. "It bothered me," Cara said. "It bothered me because I know I will never have my sister to play with again and there will never be any more of our pictures."

Michael David Uhl, now nineteen, reflects on the first anniversary of his brother's death. He went to the cemetery with his girl friend to pay his respects to Danny. "I didn't cry there, but I cry at other times. I get bitter when I see a lot of the scum and trash that walk around and think of why they are here and Danny isn't. My emotions run the gamut—bitterness, hatred, sorrow, joy—I know he was such a beautiful kid. I think of all the good times, too. I want to have happy memories of him as well as the sad ones. And then I try to remember the funny and stupid things because I want to treasure all the memories."

After Danny had been in the hospital for several days, it appeared he was improving. But one morning Michael answered the telephone and learned that his brother had taken a turn for the worse. "I knew after that phone call he was dead. I don't know why, but I just knew it. My mother didn't think of it, and I knew she wasn't expecting it, but I couldn't get rid of this feeling that Danny was already gone. When we got to his room at the hospital, there was a big green curtain around the bed. I had seen this in the movies, and at first my reaction was: 'Huh? What?' It was like being on two different planes—a weird feeling of it's something you read in the newspaper or see on television, but on another level it was me looking at this green curtain around the bed. You go from playing ball with a kid, and five days later he is dead."

Later Michael was gratified that Danny had those five days. "People came from everywhere to see him while he was in the hospital. They came from Texas to New York, and my mother's friend even came from Paris, France, to see Danny. I'm glad he had them." Michael's first instinct was to protect his mother from her grief. "Right away I had to be strong for my mother." In the next few weeks after the funeral Michael kept constantly on the run. "I ran away from the house, just to keep busy. I was in such fear of being alone and having to think about Danny. But there comes a time when you have to face it right up front. He was gone. Then come all the rotten feelings. Last year, when I had my graduation, I had only four tickets to the graduation. My mother, my father, my grandmother, and my girl friend were there, but there was no ticket for Danny. And now, a year later, I keep wishing Danny had been there. But in my heart I know that I am trying hard to be the person Danny can be proud of and I can be proud of. I know Danny would be proud of me just as I would be proud of him if I had died. And because I believe in survival after life, I expect to toss that ball around again with my brother in yet another dimension. And then I will smile. And he will, too."

Ruth Zarchin recalls when both her husband, Sam, and her brother, Bernard, were in the armed forces during World War II. Handsome, wanting to defend his country, admired and loved by all who knew him, Bernard Lichenstein was eighteen when he enlisted in the navy. He was nineteen when he was killed on an ammunition ship somewhere in the Pacific. The ship was called the *Mount Hood*. It had stopped near an island. Some of the men went ashore. Bernard stayed on the ship. It blew up. No one knew what caused the incident. The War Department sent Sarah and Sol Lichenstein a telegram that said their son was missing in action.

Sam Zarchin was stationed near San Francisco when Bernard was killed. Ruth was with her husband at that time. When she heard the news about her brother, she couldn't believe it. "I kept dreaming about him at night, that he was knocking on our door. I would open it, and he would be standing there. It is very hard to accept something like that." The effect of her brother's death on her parents is indelibly stamped in Ruth's memory. "My mother never got over his death. If we went to a movie with my parents, I would look at her and she would be crying. When we came home, I remember we would be talking to her, and suddenly she would say, 'I am going out to look for Bernard.' She would go outside and start walking. She kept hoping he would come home someday. Daddy wrote letters to senators and people in the War Department. He also found out the names of the men who went ashore that day. He wrote to them in an effort to find out what happened. He received a lot of letters, but they didn't shed any light on what really happened." Eventually Sarah and Sol received a telegram saying Bernard was killed.

After her mother and father passed away, Ruth and Sam moved into her parents' home. Ruth found a notebook. "It was full of letters that Mother had written to Bernard, after he was killed. She never mailed them. He died in 1944. She lived until 1966. Some of these letters were written right before she died."

When I corresponded with Ruth Zarchin about this book and her brother, she wrote: "I want to say again that I think it is wonderful that you thought about him." Indeed, Ruth, we all think about Bernard. We think about him, and about all the boys and men who gave their lives for their country.

In talking about her son Michael with her surviving children, Judith Haimes observed their differing reactions, from the youngest to the oldest.

Ian was one year old just three months before Michael was killed. It took Ian weeks before he wouldn't run around calling out, "Mike, Mike." On the day Michael died, just as he was leaving the house, he turned to his mother and said, "Mom, listen to this." Michael wanted Judith to hear the first word he had taught Ian to say. It was "Mike." Michael played the piano well, and he would let Ian come up to the piano and play with him. Several weeks after Michael's death, the song "The Music Box" was playing on the radio. Michael had played that tune on the piano very often. As soon as Ian heard this music coming through the radio, he went running toward the piano in the living room, hollering, "Mike, Mike." This was a child who was only one year old. Several months later Judith showed Ian a picture of Michael, but she is sure that Ian does not remember Michael at all now. What she is also sure of, however, is that Ian will be a little more confident as an adult because he was given so much love and so much affection by a brother whom he will know only through a photograph. For Michael had played with Ian, kissed him, hugged him, was very proud of him, and used to call him "little bruvver."

Joshua was three years old when his brother died. Michael had changed Joshua, given him bottles in the night, had spent a tremendous amount of time with his younger brother. Joshua knows and understands that Michael is no longer here. In the beginning he would just wander around, asking, "When is Michael coming home? Where is Michael?" After a while he began saying things like "Michael is dead. Michael's in the sky. Michael is up there with Superman." Judith and Allen tried to explain that Michael was dead, that Michael was with God. Even though Joshua is an intelligent little boy, it is very hard to explain this to a three-year-old child. One day Joshua asked his mother, "Why did God kill Michael?" Judith explained God had not killed Michael. God was taking care of Michael. Michael had been killed by a car. A little while later Joshua said, "Michael's coming back. He'll be back pretty soon. God's going to fix him up and make him all better. God can do everything."

As Judith indicates, it is hard for a three-year-old to understand that death in this form is final, that it is forever. And even when parents say all the right things, it is still final and forever. But Judith believes Joshua will always know there was a Michael. There have been times when out of the clear blue sky Joshua is in an elated mood and just starts talking about Michael. "I miss Michael. When is Michael coming home?" And then there are dejected moments when he says things like "Michael is not coming home anymore."

Jakey, the Haimeses' youngest daughter, was riding in the car with her mother one day and suddenly began speaking about the recent murders of so many children in Atlanta, Georgia. Jakey started to ask questions about what would happen if she were kidnapped. Dramatically she described how she would kick and scream and fight off her assailants. Judith turned to her young daughter and said, "Oh, Jakey, please! Don't even say such a thing because, God forbid, if I lost one more of my children, I could never live. I would never make it." And then, out of the mouth of this wise nine-year-old child came the admonition "Mom, how can *you* say such a thing! What about Ian and Joshua and Lorrie and Bobby? Mom, if anything happened to me, if the same thing happened to me that happened to Michael, you would have to live for the other children. It wouldn't be their fault if I got killed!" Jakey's keen, introspective view really brought Judith down a couple of notches. "It made me realize how very smart your children are and how really dumb you are." Judith feels it may be years, even a lifetime, before Jakey will have scars of Michael's death that are not visible. When Michael was buried, Jakey asked that a snowflake she had made be put into his coffin. This was done in accordance with her wishes. At Thanksgiving time Jakey took a little gold pin, her favorite, and put it with a note she had written to her brother: "Dear Michael. Today is Thanksgiving. Last year you were here with us. I miss you so much and I hurt so bad that you are gone. Joshua is getting very big, and Ian just had a haircut. And I love you," signed "Jakey." She asked her mother and father if the note could be put into Michael's coffin, just as the snowflake had been as an earlier remembrance of her caring and affection.

Bobby, nineteen, was away at school in Pennsylvania when

he learned of his brother's death. He took it very badly. When he heard his father's voice on the phone telling him that Michael was gone, he began to scream and cry. Bobby and Michael were typical siblings with all the rivalry that brothers have. They were very competitive. Anything Bobby could do, Michael would always try to do better, and Bobby always tried very hard to outdo anything Michael did. And they always had nasty things to say to each other. "Why don't you go comb your hair?" "You've got garlic breath. Get out of here." This continued even until the boys were nineteen and sixteen. Bobby couldn't be home for Hanukkah in December. So he had celebrated it early on his school break, which was about three weeks before Michael died. The family had had an evening for Bobby to get all his Hanukkah gifts from everyone. Michael gave his present to Bobby last. And of course, Michael told Bobby, "I want you to know I spent my last seven dollars on this. I spent only three fifty on Mom. I spent more on you than I spent on anybody." Michael's gift to Bobby was a T-shirt with a special saying imprinted on it: "That's right, pal." It was an expression Bobby used all the time. And on the reverse side of the shirt was the name of a horse Bobby had picked out to win the prestigious Woodrow Wilson race that year, Foreign Legion. Michael had scraped up the rest of his change to have the horse's name written on back of Bobby's T-shirt. But what it really said was: "Hey, Bob, I value your opinion. And I guess you're really right, so I am putting the name of the horse you chose over the name of the horse I chose on your shirt." Bobby was so taken aback by this touching gesture that for the first time since they had been young children three or four years old, when Michael reached over and kissed Bobby, instead of Bobby's pulling back and screaming as he might normally do, Bobby kissed Michael back. At that moment their dad took a photograph—a priceless photograph.

A short time later Bobby came home between school terms.

The family did a lot of reminiscing about Michael. Bobby told how Michael had been teaching him to drive the stick shift car a week before he was killed. Bobby, big and strong, did not cry much, however. He said he found it hard to cry. He felt the pain but just couldn't release tears. His mother sympathetically described her son's plight. "You have to picture Bobby, my football player, six-three, two hundred five pounds. Big boys don't cry." Several months later, when Bobby again came home on vacation, he saw a picture of Michael in his parents' bedroom. Next to it was a beautiful and poignant poem his father had written about Michael and had given to Judith on her birthday. When Bobby saw the picture of his brother and read the poem, he broke down and cried. He came out a little later and told Judith, "Mom, this is the first time I have really cried from my gut since Michael has been gone. But don't think that because the tears don't come out of my eyes the pain isn't in my heart." Bobby is back at school, working out hard for sports. Not a day goes by, he says, that he doesn't think about his brother.

Lorrie, who was twenty-one shortly after Michael died, had given him a gold watch for his fifteenth birthday. It had cost her a great deal of money. When she presented the watch to Michael, Lorrie teased him by saying she couldn't afford to buy him expensive presents very often and then showed her brother the inscription. It read: "From 15 to 25." Although Michael wore that watch everywhere he went, strangely enough, on the day he died he had taken it off and left it on his dresser.

Michael and Lorrie were very close. They were friends. They played tennis together, went to the movies together. They liked each other—as much as siblings can. Judith remembers that Michael probably summed it up best. "I like Lorrie a lot now that she doesn't live at home anymore. I wouldn't like her as much if she still lived here."

Judith Haimes describes her eldest daughter, prior to Michael's death, as having been a hyper, high-strung child, extremely emotional, one who would cry at a parade. "Lorrie would cry taking her soda bottles back to the store." She had a tendency to be wrapped up in herself sometimes. But amazing things took place in Lorrie when she learned her brother had died. She saw her parents crumbling, so she took over. She went to the car in which her brother had been killed and took out his personal belongings. When she saw that her parents could not face it, Lorrie even went to pick up the police report. She did all the necessary jobs that had to be done and never complained. She cried, and she grieved, and she still does. But her parents have noticed a great maturity and strength in their daughter. Now, when she calls her mother and father, she asks, "Mom, how are *you* feeling? Dad, how are *you* feeling?" She has put her parents first in an amazing way. She has her own grief but keeps it to herself or shares it with the boy she is going to marry—someone who is sympathetic and to whom she can talk. She tries not to add her grief to that of her parents.

Judith believes there will come a time when they all can sit down as a family and say, "Let's talk about it together and cry together." But they are not yet ready for that. They are not ready to see each other cry and fall apart because it is still too new.

7 · The Male Viewpoint

The bereaved father suffers severely in the lonely pew of suppressed grief. He endures not only the psychological impact of losing his child but the fear of losing his masculine identity by publicly displaying his distress. In building an image to fit what our society expects, a man who openly reveals his emotions during a time of tragedy feels he is looked down upon in most quarters. We are taught to expect a "real" man to be strong in time of crisis, strong in time of war, strong under fire. But what society does not fathom is that the loss of a child doesn't rank with other stress emotions. The loss of one's child transcends the barrier of do's and don'ts for emotional behavior. The honest gut emotion of cleansing the soul with tears of grief is akin to lancing a wound to drain the infection. A man *or* a woman is entitled to the right of expiating sorrow.

Men should be made aware that it is a natural response for them to experience the same emotional upheaval in grieving the death of a child that women do. In suffering a loss of such magnitude, it is also natural—and *not* unmasculine—for a man to find himself dealing with periods of anger, guilt, moroseness, anxiety, frustration, and other real and gnawing thoughts. Grieving is a period of adjustment—for men as well as women. Many fathers refrain from acknowledging that they continue to experience this grief in the belief they have to mask their feelings, to hide them from view lest they be considered weak or unmanly. In so doing, they commit a great injustice to themselves. For, like the octaves on a piano, a real man should be able to display emotions in any range and grow from them.

Leo C. Lefebvre, Jr., was one such father. His tears came when his son, his first born, died, a victim of Sudden Infant Death Syndrome:

After frantic resuscitation attempts at home and a high-speed ambulance ride to the hospital, my wife and I were left in an emergency room amid much confusion both within ourselves and within the hospital. When we were told by a nurse that our son was dead, I reacted with the feelings deep within my inner being and began to cry uncontrollably. Evidently those around me couldn't cope with tears from a man and before I knew it, I was being shot in both arms. The sedation placed me in a state of unreality for a while, but it really didn't do anything about the way I felt. How could it? It only prevented me from expressing my true feelings. I had to deal with them later.

While attending a counseling conference workshop, Leo was in a group discussion with three couples who had lost children to Sudden Infant Death Syndrome. The input from the men was extremely enlightening:

One of the fathers admitted that even though two years had passed, he was still unable to talk much about their baby's death. Another father immediately offered a comment that he had similar feelings. His wife responded with amazement, "I didn't know that you felt that way! Why didn't you tell me?" This couple had lost their infant almost five years ago. One cannot help thinking of the many destructive things that may have been going on inside these fathers for long periods of time. It's all so unnecessary.

Leo Lefebvre found he couldn't deal with himself after the death of his son. He rushed back to work, thinking if he occupied himself by keeping busy, he wouldn't have to face the realities. "Well, let me tell you it was back at work I first began to think, feel, and deal with my grief. *It is extremely important for a man to be able to tell his wife how he feels at work.* I found myself staring into space, not able to concentrate, getting angry. I took pains to avoid facing people and the probing questions they asked. I found that there was an extremely painful, difficult, uncomfortable job to be performed inside myself.

This job was even more difficult than the initial mourning. A part of me was lost in my son, along with all the expectations I had for our lives together."

Leo feels a man may often hold in his grief and painful thoughts for fear of losing control if he lets go. "He has trouble identifying feelings of grief and does not know how to deal with them alone. Sometimes it is hard for him to understand really just what is going on inside himself. Feelings inside a person are similar to a dam filling with water. Finally, a point is reached where the dam cannot hold any more water, and the water bursts forth, destroying everything in its path. If the water level had been controlled and allowed to run out a little at a time, things may have gotten wet but would not have been destroyed. So it is with our feelings—for women and for men."

Leo stresses that parents should realize there is nothing one can do to eliminate the pain associated with the loss of a child. "But there are many things that can be done to help parents express their grief in a healthy, constructive way. Paramount is the encouragement of parents to communicate their true feelings to each other no matter how awkward or crazy they may seem at the time."

Death didn't become a real part of Leo's life until he lost his firstborn, a son, to SIDS. Since that time he has experienced the death of a second son and close relatives. He has observed that grandparents have a double reaction to the death of your child. "They react not only to the death of a grandchild but to the grief of their own child. I wish that there were easy answers on what to do for grandparents to resolve their grief feelings, but there really aren't any specific answers. There are too many variables. We are basically still a death-denying society. Sometimes superstitious statements or beliefs, though well intended, may be devastating or destructive to the couple. This may cause a barrier to be placed between the couple and the grandparents. One solution is to keep the channels of communication open for a free exchange of information and a sharing of feelings. Don't try to force issues. I know that many grandparents still can't talk about their SIDS [Sudden Infant Death Syndrome, or crib death] loss. Because of this, they may seem uncomfortable and throw up roadblocks when the subject matter is approached."

Leo offers his thoughts only as a guide to a father's feelings. "There cannot be an absolute, correct, or ideal way to deal with loss." He states that not all fathers will react the same way, nor will they necessarily be able to identify with what Leo has shared with us. "Just as each father is similar but different, so then are each father's feelings and reactions to the death of his child." Leo is also concerned about suppressed thoughts men have. "Some fathers have told me it goes something like this: 'I left for work in the morning, and the baby was fine. I got a call to come quick and found the baby dead. What happened?' The answer that nothing had happened kept coming back. 'Then why is my baby dead?' No one knows. Although this is not expressed openly, the husband may indirectly and subconsciously blame his wife. The blame may manifest itself later in many ways. *This is pure dynamite and must surface immediately, to be confronted and dealt with constructively. The air needs to be cleared on this matter quickly so that this blaming doesn't have a chance to grow or become destructive.*" Leo believes such inner feelings by the husband set up tremendous conflicts. "He loves his wife but may indirectly hold her responsible for the death of their baby. He may have to be told and convinced not only by his wife but by others in authority there was nothing his wife did or didn't do that caused the death of their baby." This problem may be more prevalent in SIDS deaths. This largest killer of infants, often in the first months of life, occurs silently and mysteriously in the home. It occurs without warning in infants who have been perceived as healthy and wreaks havoc on the 1 in 350 parents who also become its victims.

At a time when parents are devastated, Leo urges neighbors to be supportive—and to continue that support. "Neighbors may fall into two groups: one, *supportive* in a warm but awkward sort of way because of their fears and reactions to death; and two, *isolating* because of their fear that whatever killed your child was contagious or because of a reluctance to get involved. In the case of supportive neighbors, the SIDS parents usually must initiate the conversation. Neighbors who feel they just don't know what to do for you or what to say may stay away. They may be fearful of upsetting you by saying or doing something wrong. As a result, SIDS parents may feel isolated. It's an uncomfortable, lonely position to be in. My advice to neighbors is to reach out, however awkward it may seem. Let the parents know you care deeply about their loss and you are there with them. A thoughtful neighbor can lend much support to a grieving family often in very practical ways, such as providing child care or meals."

Leo indicates situations will occur that entail parents meeting people who do not know your child has died. He tells of one such instance that happened to him and his wife. "One of the couples we had met through childbirth classes stopped by to visit us about two weeks after we had lost our son. It was apparent they didn't know. My wife and I just sat there, waiting for the inevitable question—the time bomb to go off. They had brought their son with them and after a while innocently asked if our son was taking a nap. When we told them what had happened, we had to comfort them." As their life begins to return to a semblance of routine, parents start to face uncomfortable encounters. Leo urges facing them as they occur, one at a time. "Parents must begin the long, hard road back to reality. Situations such as this are bound to occur as your life begins to return to a routine. My life has changed in so many ways in the years since Peter's death. I still think about my son and think of what could have been had he lived. More important, life seems more precious to me now. Four lively children have been added to our family. I have grown to love in a deeper way and feel better prepared to reach out with that love. I now know that I am my brother's keeper."

Leo urges counselors to become aware of fathers' feelings.

"Counselors are too often accustomed to dealing with mothers. They should make special efforts to include and welcome fathers in counseling sessions. The husband and wife are on a teeter-totter. When one is up, the other is down. The overly strong silent husband may have a wife who has to express the pain for both. The wife, on the other hand, may appear so depressed that the husband does not dare risk revealing that he too needs help. Counselors should be aware that many times they need to give parents permission to express pain, usually in the form of tears. Counselors should also point out that tears are not the only signs of grief."

It is important to realize grief is a process that must be gone through. "We grow according to how we experience this process," Leo states. "There is no healthy way around it—only through it."

Dr. Peter Purpura, whose eight-year-old daughter Cassandra died of a brain tumor, was angry at the insensitive lack of attention to a bereaved father. "Most people, even friends, will call and never ask me how I am doing. They ask how Angela is. It's as if my wife is supposed to have a reaction to the loss of our child, but I am not, and I find it drives me bananas—that you are a man and not supposed to be upset with these things. It's not viewed as the same loss."

Not only has Peter known the anguish of a bereaved father, but he also suffers the anxiety of having only one child now. There is a terror of something happening to her. Too, he feels that everything with his surviving daughter is tainted. "There is always that sense of whatever happens, this didn't happen to Cassandra or isn't happening with Cassandra. If Cara gets promoted or when she gets married, all these things are going to have an edge to them that they didn't have before."

But while Peter agonized with such fearful thoughts, it was not an easy task to express them to others. Even a friend for whom Peter had been best man was not privy to his inner feelings, for they had grown apart over the years. When they met accidentally shortly after Cassandra died, Peter did not even mention her death. At the same time Peter tells of another meeting with a relative stranger. "I met a fellow on the train whose daughter had been in my daughter's class. That really was the only basis for our knowing each other. He asked me how I was doing, and I gave him a very glib answer. But he pursued it, and I opened up and spent about forty-five minutes *really* telling him how I was feeling." It was a catharsis for Peter, and he was comfortable in talking because of the man's sincerity.

Peter has observed in other bereaved couples that often a wife will say about her mate, "Well, you know, he doesn't cry. He doesn't deal with things the way I do," only to have the husband quickly state, "But I do. I just don't cry in front of you." Peter believes it is much harder for men to be supportive of each other, that men are afraid of showing their emotions to each other. "There is the sense that the man is supposed to protect his wife and is supposed to take care of her." Peter's wife has observed that a large percentage of fathers—approximately one-third to one-half—attend meetings at their chapter of The Compassionate Friends (this organization will be described later). Angela believes Peter's mere presence at the meeting—as a bereaved father who is unafraid of expressing his raw emotions—and what he is able to contribute verbally are of great importance to the men. "Fathers are able to open up and cry at our meetings. I do not think you would see men cry elsewhere, at least, not as readily. But they feel comfortable in doing so because they know Peter has been there, and that we understand."

Reflecting about his feelings concerning the meetings, Peter took pen in hand and recorded some of his thoughts:

Damn it. It is Friday, another meeting tonight. How I hate those meetings. They are so painful. I remember the first one:

going around the room, all that pain. I never really wanted to go. She dragged me. I am going for her. On the way home it hit me. We aren't alone. So many have lost children. Everyone killed in a war has left parents behind to bury and grieve. All those people in the same boat. Since time began, parents have had to face their children dying. How strange; I never thought of that, never considered it. No one has ever lost a child in my family. But Aunt Connie died when she was twenty. Maybe that is why Grandma always seemed so sad. And Dad's cousin lost a little girl to a brain tumor, just like Cassandra.

Why do we go to these meetings? I dread them. There will be pain. New people wiped out and unable to speak. God, we were once like that; just all raw, all the time. It is better now. We can even joke at times. Some days are even good. It has been hard. We have been ripped open, and we must heal. It is easy to heal the surface, to cover it over. To let it heal from the inside, to cope with the depths of the pain, to experience the hurt—that makes it heal differently. There will always be a scar, something missing. Coping and feeling, they can fuse things, make them stronger. A break in a bone can mend and be the strongest part of the bone. Maybe this can heal and be the strongest part of us. To make a healed wound a living memory to our child. To let it fuse, layer upon layer, with all the pain that it takes.

She was such a blessing and a joy; that she touched my life is so important. The few years she was here were so important to me. She was part of my family. God, she was precious. I go and I remember. I dread remembering. I hate the insensitivity we speak of, as it is salt on the wounds we carry. Some days are so bad; some are good now.

After the meeting I feel better. It sounds strange. How can that be? But it is. Sheila was so upset that one meeting. She said she won't ever come back. Ernie said we should stop talking about friends and speak of our own losses. Then he didn't come the next month, and we took his advice anyway. It was so hard, but Sheila said more to me that night about her son than she ever had and she looked better. How strange, so pained she doesn't want to return, and she looks better. It was a terrible meeting. How strange I feel better. I don't really understand this, but thank God for it.

Peter has observed the problems of surviving male children. "The boys have a commitment that they are supposed to tough this out, that they are not to be upset about it, that they are not supposed to talk about it. I think this carries right down to the younger kids. And I think the younger they are, the harder it is because they are still struggling with what it means to be a man. It's harder for them to go against what they are supposed to do than it is for people who are older."

When asked if he had any suggestions to help men convey their emotions, Peter responded, "As a bereaved parent, my feeling is that a man has no more responsibility to protect his wife than she does to take care of him. The fact of the matter is that what has hit you has hit *both* of you. And to take on the responsibility of having to protect your wife in that situation is really to take on more than you really can handle. A man is not supposed to have a reaction. It's incredibly consistent."

Peter also has some suggestions to offer the clergy in working with bereaved parents. A clinical psychologist and psychoanalyst, Peter does not speak from that point of view, but from that of a bereaved father: "It seems that the clergy may be too pressed to take on the role of sharing with the bereaved. However, their unique position in the community and in the lives of their congregation make them most valuable as a source of comfort and support. For people to hear from a man of God that we cannot understand the ways of God can be of great help in the first step away from the tormenting question 'Why has my child died?'

"Patience and support may help bereaved people avoid the disastrous dead end of blaming God for the death of a child and help the bereaved parent come to see that we must accept the fact of the death and that it will never be clear why this happened.

"Our responsibility is to make the best of what has occurred to us and this is a responsibility to God and to ourselves. This message I feel comes best from the clergy. In addition to an ear, providing the comfort and support of sharing pain is the greatest gift a clergyman can offer. The work involved in this is not to be underestimated. To share someone's pain is to put yourself through it at least in part. The effect of this on the listener is marked and may be the reason why many stay away from working with the bereaved.

"The service provided by clergy in officiating at wakes and funerals of our dead children is an enormous service. The comfort of ceremonies, the support of the structure of the institution, and the traditional wisdom of religious practice are all a help to those who can utilize them. Many agnostic members in The Compassionate Friends have expressed envy for those who can utilize faith and religion as a vehicle for coping with grief.

"In your dealing with bereaved parents, it is important not to be caught up by justifying the death as God's will or being pressed to explain why. However, much anger may be directed at you as a man of God. If it is any consolation, the medical profession comes out much worse as the object of the anger of bereaved parents. This anger is a very basic part of early grief, and like the storm, it must be weathered. What excuse people give for being angry is usually just a rationalization. They are just angry with reality.

"Later the listening and sharing of the hurt take over. If this is combined with prayer, it seems to me this could be especially helpful for those who are so inclined. It is necessary to be flexible and take direction from the bereaved person, for insensitive reactions can make things worse rather than better, and many are driven away from their religion when this occurs."

Fred Wiener's daughter, Frances, age thirty-one, was killed in a car crash while out on a date. Fred received a telephone call from Boston, where his daughter was residing. Friends of Frances told him the tragic news. Fred's wife, Edith, was in Florida. "Believe it or not, my first thoughts were: 'How am I going to break this to my wife?' She was a war widow when I married her. Her first husband had been killed in the Battle of the Bulge. She had lost a twenty-eight-year-old brother. She had also lost her parents and a sister. And now we had this: our only daughter." Fred and Edith had a surviving son and two grandchildren. His son was away for the weekend, so Fred was alone. Neighbors came and stayed with him. His brother-in-law and his wife's sister also arrived to help. Fred could not bring himself to tell his wife on the phone. He could not trust his emotions, either, to talk to her. And so his brother-in-law said he would telephone Edith. He told her Fred was ill with a kidney stone. Edith became alarmed that they were hiding from her the fact that Fred had had a heart attack. At this point Fred got on the phone to reassure her he was not that ill. But he began to cry, and Edith wanted to know what was wrong. Fred told her it was just the pain from the kidney stone. Edith arrived home the next morning. Upon learning the actual news, she could not be consoled. "My wife became suicidal. She didn't want to keep going. After *shiva,* which we sit in the Jewish religion for seven days, I went back to work to keep busy. But I wouldn't go unless someone stayed with my wife. She began to go to a private therapist. Then we began to go to a bereavement center and later we went to The Compassionate Friends."

There was a division of feelings about God in the couple's relationship. "I feel closer to God. I am hoping that there is an afterworld and I can see my daughter again. But my wife feels there can't be a God if He let this happen. People told us that our daughter had done so much good helping others that God wanted her. That didn't help my wife. The only way we kept going was I displayed as much affection as I could. I told her how much I needed her. Also, the presence of our grandchildren and the fact that we had a surviving child helped us. A lot of people said the wrong things. In going to The Compassionate Friends' meetings and also in group therapy, we learned that people don't know how to express themselves. They avoid talking to you. They feel guilty that their kids are okay and you had this terrible tragedy."

Fred would become angry when people would ask him, "How is your wife doing?" He felt pain. He was hurting, too. "They would never ask how the husband is. When you go to meetings, you hear other men say this same thing, and it is so wrong, so unfair. A husband feels it just as much as the wife. He grieves, too. I have seen couples where the wife keeps the husband going. And husbands become susceptible to illnesses just the way the wives do. There are a lot of physical problems that occur because your resistance is low from emotional strain, exhaustion, and the fatigue of trying to live when your child is dead."

Abe Malawski remembers when he came back from the cemetery after burying his older son, he worried about the impact on his younger son, Steven. "I wanted to make sure that he understood he was loved no less than his brother. There had been an enormous number of people attending the funeral services. Anyone would have been impressed at this tremendous turnout for paying respect to my son. I wanted to be sure my surviving son knew, after seeing these enormous crowds there for his brother, that this had no bearing on our love for him. In the kitchen I put my arms around Steven and we both started to cry. I said to him, 'Steven, just remember one thing: I love you very much, and I don't love you any less because of your brother. I loved your brother because he was Harvey, and I love you because you are Steven. One has nothing to do with the other.' Steven's answer to me was: 'I know, Dad.' I never wanted Steven to say, 'Hey, world, I am here, too!' Steven is as much of my world as Harvey."

Abe tells of the change that takes place after the death of a child. "The heart and the mind don't come together on a thing like this. You are dealing with such an unnatural happening. All your plans become disconnected. You have projects with your future, and most of your goals are for your children. You figure whatever years you have left, you want to get dividends from your children when and if they get married and have their children. You like to brag about their accomplishments and what they did in life. When you lose a child, you lose all that. As somebody said, 'When you lose a child, you lose your future.' "

Abe strongly feels it takes someone who has lost a child to know what losing a child is. "I hear people tell me about their losses, and I turn them off. They just don't know what they are talking about. When people tell me they have lost parents or an aunt or another member of the family and are trying to make me feel good, I listen with half an ear. They simply do not know what a bereaved parent feels, what losing a child means. I wish, if they want to make me feel good, that they wouldn't say anything. It is easier. Because you cannot compare apples and oranges. To me, if they say nothing, it is better. If they squeeze my hand or squeeze my shoulder, they are saying much more. First of all, there are no words in our vocabulary to tell you, 'I feel sorry for what happened.' Don't say anything. Hold me, instead. Let me have the warmth of your body. Embracing someone says more. At least to me it has more meaning. One friend said to me, 'I lost my wife, and it was terrible. You have to give yourself time.' But in the meantime, he forgets he has remarried. He has found another person to share his love. But I can never replace my child. You can have fifteen children, and it will make no difference. You can never replace a child."

Abe tells of a poignant moment when two bereaved parents danced for the first time:

"In December, we decided for the first time to accept an invitation to a social gathering. The son of one of Judy's co-workers had gotten married a year ago and lived out of state. He came in with his wife, and his mother had a gathering to which we were invited. We went with some trepidation. While we had gone out to restaurants to eat, this was the first time we got dressed to go out to a function. When we arrived, we heard music. There was a band. It was the first time that Judy's co-workers had seen me other than in the setting where they met me—at the sitting of *shiva*. This was nine months later. They all came over and were very effusive and glad to see us at a 'happy' occasion. The band was playing something slow. I happen to like to dance, but all kinds of questions and thoughts were running through my mind: 'I feel like dancing, but I feel guilty. I don't know how Judy is going to react.' Finally, I asked her, 'Would you like to dance?' Her answer was, 'If you want to.' So, I said, 'Okay.' Later, I found out she felt guilty too. But we danced, and it felt good to dance. Eventually, we allowed ourselves to have a good time without feeling guilty about it, because the second dance was easier than the first, and the third dance was easier than the second and the first."

Yet, two weeks later, there was a Christmas party at Abe's place of business that caused him to break down. "I went to pieces because everyone was laughing. Everyone was having a good time—but it was a different kind of a good time. Everyone was saying, 'Have a happy New Year. Have a healthy New Year.' That went against everything in me—to tell me to be happy when I was crying inside. The day foreman saw me. He came over and cradled me in his arms. I don't remember what he said, but the essence of it was, 'It's all right. It's okay to cry.' "

It distresses Abe that most men feel they are supposed to hide their feelings. "You are not supposed to cry if you are a man. And I don't go along with that. I am normally emotional. I lost so much—how can I bury it? That I have been able to cry has helped me. And after I cry, I feel better."

Mark Andrew Freireich, age seventeen, was in an automobile accident on February 5, 1975. He died on May 24 of that year. Ernie Freireich describes his feelings: "To see my son in a coma and to watch him die slowly was excruciating pain—feelings that parents can't put into words. Each night at home I would sob myself to sleep." Ernie feels that in a world that expects the macho image, showing emotion is taken as losing control. He remembers trying to maintain an exterior cover, trying to function at work and at home.

Ernie tells of the different stresses a bereaved parent experiences. "In a state of bereavement you really are in a state of depression. All your values in life are changing. You wake up in the morning crying. You go to bed crying. You walk around with clenched jaws. After a while you realize that your jaw hurts, your arms ache, your stomach hurts—because you are in a state of stress."

Family arguments become more acute. "You are taxing any relationship because there is no tolerance when you are so emotionally weakened. With things that once seemed minor, you can no longer contain your temper. You become angry easily. Everything is an insult. If the faucet is leaking and you haven't fixed it, this is taken as a personal insult. She feels you don't realize how she is suffering. And vice versa. Everything is disproportionate. It's like two beginning skaters who go out to skate for the first time. They are least capable of helping each other because they both are continuously falling."

Parents feel such a sense of helplessness. "It drives people to examine their personal values, their philosophy, their religion." Ernie believes that in the initial impact of the shock of your child's death, nature plays a role. "It puts you in a fog because you cannot cope at the time. It is nature's way of protecting you so you don't lose control. For it is here that there exists a fine line between sanity and insanity. It is delicately balanced by the stupor nature protects you with, acting as a way of anesthetizing the pain. Three or four weeks afterward, when friends and relatives are no longer around to be supportive, reality sets in. The reality is that you must accept not only your child's death but part of your own death. What we do for most of life is to cover the reality of our own demise. That terror of death is in every one of us. Then, when it is forced into your home, you are ill equipped to handle it."

Seven years after his son's death Ernie reflects that many parents feel extended bereavement is necessary as a tribute to their child. Ernie has observed that often parents believe the longer they grieve, the longer they are symbolizing their love. "But this is an impairment to recovery. You will always love your child. You don't have to serve a lifetime sentence to prove it."

Ernie also cautions parents about the devastating effect continued grief has on surviving children. "What you are saying in prolonged grief is: 'My world has ended.' That is the message parents are sending if they go on and on with their grief. The surviving child wonders, 'Don't I mean anything to you?' Many times parents tend to idealize the dead child, and for that reason siblings often feel the child who died was the favorite." He urges parents to reconstruct their lives in the knowledge that others need them.

Allen Haimes still has moments when he can't believe his son is dead. He is constantly telling himself, "Michael is dead. He is really dead." He says it often to shock himself, to try to accept the reality. One of the things that helped Allen the most came from someone he knew only slightly, a father who had lost a two-year-old daughter in a drowning accident the previous year. The father lived nearby, and when he and his wife heard about Michael, they came to comfort the Haimeses. The father spoke to Allen on a one-to-one basis. "You think you will never smile again. You think you will never laugh again, but you will. It just takes time." This father had no motive other than to try to reach out and help another father to get beyond where Allen was. And he did. Allen *has* laughed since that time, and he *has* partially resumed a normal existence.

Nine months after the death of his son Allen Haimes's emotions were still of a roller-coaster nature. He would get waves of extensive pain, thinking back on all the good times he and his son had enjoyed together. "I miss him. I miss him a whole lot. The reality that we won't have any of those times together again makes me feel I want to scream." But Allen gets beyond these setback moments by concentrating on exclusively positive times together.

It was very difficult for Allen Haimes when he first returned to his dental practice. "As soon as the scab formed, every half hour it was ripped off," he said. Ten times a day ten different patients would come in and say, "Gee, Doc, I was sorry to hear about your son." Then they would ask questions, thinking probably that since Allen was back at work, he was "holding up." Later, though, when Allen was involved with a root canal or a surgical procedure, even for those few minutes when he was deeply involved with something mechanical, he was granted relief from thinking about his dead son. His body, his soul, and his mind had blessed relief, if only for those few minutes, from that excruciating, consuming pain. Allen feels it is important to return to work, to resume some normal activity, even if it is just going to the supermarket. You might be in agony, but you are bearing up. And, for just those few minutes when the checker is telling you how much your groceries are costing and you are looking for your wallet, for those precious minutes you are not thinking about your son. It may not seem like much to someone who has not lost a child, but to someone who *has* lost a child, those few minutes without pain are relief beyond measure.

Basically Allen views the whole thing as "going left to right." He believes you can either grow from an experience like this, and become extremely positive, or become extremely negative. Allen Haimes chose to become positive. He wants to make Mike's life count. "I want to incorporate the essence of what he was about into the other children, into our lives, into my future goals, and make his life, and what he was about, count, so that it doesn't die and it doesn't end with death."

Sidney Davis is a consulting electrical engineer whose son was slain when he surprised burglars at the family's home. Twelve days following the murder New York police charged two suspects with the robbery and murder. One of the suspects, who were drug addicts, appeared to be more callous than the other, but at one point in the questioning a detective put something in front of this hard-shelled suspect. That something was a copy of a letter written by the father of the murdered boy, describing the family's feelings and asking the perpetrator to look at what he had done to the family. Reading Sidney Davis's letter, his shell disintegrating, the suspect confessed through tears that he had killed Norman. The confession was a contributing factor in the conviction of both suspects. Below is the text of that letter, in which Sidney Davis so poignantly expresses a father's grief and outrage.

On the afternoon of Friday, July 28, an intruder violated my home and murdered my twenty-year-old son.

When I consider the complex legal procedures in prosecuting a person for taking another's life, I marvel at the ease with which the murderer of my son cut through the red tape.

But my baby is gone, and that's all there is to that. The rituals of my Hebrew religion are now taking over, easing the spikes of pain during the transition back to an approximation of normalcy.

Nevertheless, my heart still cringes in horror at the thought of the pain and terror that he must have felt in the last minutes of his life. Nothing in our house will ever again be the same.

But as decreed by the God of my people, "Life is for the living," and I must now concentrate on restoring and maintaining the faith and strength of my sources of faith and strength, my dear wife, Barbara, and my two remaining children, Kenneth and Peter. They assured me on the night of our disaster that we have always been a strong family and that we will survive. At that time I wasn't so sure.

As expected, our relatives came from nearby and far, doing

their part to bring familiar comforts and reassurances to our home. Whatever could be done, they did.

But somewhat less expected—though as I see it now, it shouldn't have been less expected—was the comfort extended by our neighbors and acquaintances, who quietly and sensitively banded together to take care of our physical and emotional needs. Their presence helped and will help us until we can cope by ourselves with our more solitary routines.

My family now feels a deepened sense of community. Instead of regarding ourselves, as we had, primarily as visitors (for twenty-three years) from the Bronx, we now feel pride in belonging to the close-knit community of East Norwich. This new source of strength will stay with us as long as we live.

Of the "alleged perpetrator," or whatever they call murderers today, I ask:

How dare you take my child's life?
How dare you deprive his family and those who loved him?
How dare you steal, from my wife and myself, the daughter-in-law and the grandchildren my son would have brought us!
How dare you!

You were yourself once an innocent boy, but you became a tiger who eats people. How must your mother and other close relatives feel?

But it is not outrage which prompts me to affirm the obvious, that tigers must be confined and not allowed on furloughs based upon promises to kill no more. It is not really in the nature of tigers to make such promises with conviction.

My son's name was Norman—sometimes called Numo, exactly why I don't know, but the reasons are rooted in love and affection. I return the love of my family to Numo's friends, most of whom we knew.

The Davis family also thanks all the organizations who have provided us assistance, my many business friends and associates for the comfort and love they have brought us, and the police detectives who demonstrated not only competence, efficiency, and thoroughness (regardless of the outcome of the present investigation) but also sensitivity and compassion.

Before closing, I feel compelled to make an appeal. For the time being, the tiger is still loose, but his dreadful act will cause him persistent suffering as long as he lives. Those close to him, his parents, relatives, friends, and acquaintances, can diminish his suffering by urging him to come forth to be helped. Or just tell the authorities who and where he is. Such a compassionate act would not only help the tiger but may also save the life of another family's child.

8 · Friends

After the death of her eight-year-old son, Doris Young didn't want to see any of her friends. Even her best friend was not welcome.

"How could anyone understand how I was really feeling? What did people know about losing a child? What I felt was nothing they had any idea about, nothing they could possibly ever feel." Doris was angry at those she felt were patronizing her. "People kept saying things like 'God knew what he was doing.' And I didn't want to hear about God. I didn't want to hear about anything."

Doris avoided talking to people, to the extent that she often would not answer the phone. But one friend pursued it. She came to see Doris and said, "Maybe what I have been saying hasn't sat too well, but we have been friends for a very long time. Maybe there is something *you* want to say." Doris had so many mixed feelings about why the tragedy happened. She had kept everything bottled in—until this friend asked her if there was anything she wanted to say.

"That friend helped me more than anyone because I was able to pour my heart out. We had grown up together. I knew this friend loved my child, and I knew I could cry in front of her. And I did. I cried from my soul."

Abe Malawski reacts very strongly to people who can't grasp the anguish parents experience when losing a child. "The thing that galls me the most is that people seem to be afraid of us. They seem to think whatever happened to us will rub off on them. The outside world just doesn't know how to handle someone who has lost a child. If you lose a father or mother, people will pay their condolences. They accept it as part of life. But losing a child is so unnatural. First of all, children are supposed to bury their parents, not the other way around." Abe believes that in our society one makes burial provisions for oneself, parents, or family members if there is a family plot. "But you don't make burial provisions for your children. Never in your mind do you allow any room to think that your children will go before you. It's just unnatural. You become a pariah."

A source of great annoyance to Abe is that the burden of contacting friends may be left to the bereaved parents. "They all give you the same story. 'Call me when you are ready to go out. Call me when you are ready for company. Call me when you are ready for coffee and cake.' You are expected to make the first move. Or they call members of the family and ask, 'How are Abe and Judy doing?' My answer has always been: 'If they want to know, let them call and find out.'" Abe tells of meeting new people by attending meetings at The Compassionate Friends, a group of bereaved parents. "The couple who headed the group were very effective. I did very well there, but my wife cannot handle a lot of people. She cannot take crowds. At the first meeting there were fifty or sixty people present. A few months later there were close to a hundred. After the meetings we would break up into smaller groups. It was then my wife would participate. Inasmuch as I worked at night, it was difficult for me to attend the evening meetings of The Compassionate Friends. We heard about a bereavement center. My wife suggested that we go because it was once a week and the group had only twelve people. My wife doesn't talk at every meeting, but you can see her participating even by *not* saying anything. She will nod or start crying. Or tears will well up in her eyes. Every once in a while she will make comments. Everybody reacts differently. Just because my wife doesn't like crowds, who am I to tell her, 'No, you must,' when I have my own idiosyncrasies about the way I am trying to recover?"

Some months later Abe heard that The Compassionate Friends was holding a meeting on New Year's Day. "I was off from work that day and we were able to go. When we arrived, people we had met before greeted us. We hugged and kissed people. It was like meeting long-lost friends, like old home week."

Ellen Uhl lost her sixteen-year-old son when he suddenly developed an aneurysm of the aorta. Five days later Danny was dead. "During the first two weeks everyone comes. The doorbell is ringing, and each time you expect someone who will be the right person to help you. And it never is."

Ellen says friends just don't know what to do in this situation. "They look at me in a sort of compromising way, but they are *not* treating me normally." Even though there is one close friend to whom Ellen can pour her heart out, that best friend wants Ellen the way she used to be—the way she was prior to her son's death. When asked if talking to a friend helps, Ellen replied, "Nothing helps. Absolutely nothing. But if you say it—'my son died on such-and-such a day'—then it relieves you some just to have said it. From that standpoint perhaps it can be considered a help." Ellen told of a meeting she attended at The Compassionate Friends. The subject of "friends" was brought up by the group. "The head of the group is a psychoanalyst who is also a bereaved parent. He said we were complaining about our friends because we don't want to talk about the real issue that our child isn't here any longer. He was trying to help us understand our feelings, and it helped."

What Ellen would like friends and other people to say to her is: "Will it bother you if I talk to you?" She feels when people avoid her, it is the same as saying they don't want to talk to her. "I appreciate it more than anything that they just listen to me." In one instance she spoke to a friend to whom she feels close about a reaction of anger she had to another friend. She asked the friend to state her honest feeling about the incident. Her friend felt Ellen was too sensitive, and Ellen tried to reexamine her own feelings.

In most instances Ellen found it difficult to be with former friends. There had been friendships that had grown and deepened through the years when her son was growing up. There had been happy times when she and her family had celebrated special occasions with friends as a unit. She could no longer treasure these previously joyous memories. For seeing these friends and their children now brought back memories that were painfully sharp and intensified the stark reality that Ellen would never see her son again.

After their son's death Judith and Allen Haimes stayed away from people, even their close friends. What they needed most, they felt, was to be together. So that was what they did. Gradually, after a period of months, they returned to their old circle of friends. However, this proved to be a difficult period of readjustment—more so for the friends than for Judith and Allen. Judith remembers, "Some of our friends, while I can't say they avoided us, were kind of uncomfortable about how to act. 'God, can we tell a dirty joke?' 'Can we have a glass of beer?' 'Can we laugh at the movie?' " Judith and Allen did go to a movie with another couple. It was a comedy, but there was a cemetery scene in it. The other couple squirmed during this part. They seemed to be thinking: "Oh, here is a cemetery scene, and these people have just buried their son." So in the beginning most of Judith's and Allen's friends were ill at ease in their company.

"Some bereaved parents feel it is sacrilegious to talk about their child's death all the time, while others want to talk about it constantly," Judith thinks. Under the circumstances friends don't know what to do. They don't want to bring up the subject for fear of upsetting the parents, but they don't want to seem insensitive to the death either. Judith believes some of their friends stopped asking them to go to parties and movies because the friends thought: How could they enjoy themselves with their child dead a few months? Before the tragedy the Haimeses had been considered an ideal couple and family. When their son died, their friends were also in shock: "How could this happen to such a perfect couple? They were so special." Judith says, "When this terrible thing happened to us, it was as if we had to be different. We were expected to wear black forever because we had to show we were in mourning."

Judith hits upon the nerve center of what friends experience when learning of the death of a child. "These friends recognized *mortality*. If they could empathize and sympathize, if they could relate to us in any way, then they, too, would become *mortal*. And they would have to recognize that if we, their friends—ordinary people—could lose our child, then, God forbid, they could lose theirs. And how can you tell a joke to somebody when you saw that woman hysterical in a graveyard burying her son? How could anything ever be funny to her again? This is how people's minds work. Because they don't understand. I don't want to feel guilty if I laugh, if I joke, if I cry."

Judith feels it is important to give yourself time to feel angry and time to grieve but cautions against prolonged dwelling on the death of a child. "A parent gives birth to a child, and for the first three months you talk about the pregnancy. After the birth you talk about being in labor and giving birth to the child. After that you don't talk about the birth of that child anymore. You may talk about the child once in a while, but you don't dwell on the birth. You don't dwell on what it was like being pregnant. It is the same with the death of a child. After the first couple of months you stop discussing it with every person who will listen to what it was like to go through that death process with your child. You start talking about things like 'Remember when Michael fell off the bike?' Or 'Remember the time he hit the tire swing with his head?' You start talking about him like any other child you had. This is the difference between the healthy and the unhealthy. And it may help save friendships." Judith also feels parents should not overshadow the lives of their living children with reminders of the child who has died. "When the wonderful events of your surviving children's lives take place, they shouldn't be taken away from. Statements like, 'Oh, it's your graduation day; your brother would have been proud if he were here' can evoke bad connotations for the surviving child and make him feel like saying, 'What about me?' Instead of saying, 'Oh, if only your brother were here,' parents have to realize it is this child's beautiful day and they are entitled to enjoy it on their own steam. Whether the event is a graduation, a wedding, or whatever, a cloud can appear for the siblings if parents outshine their surviving children thoughtlessly."

Allen Haimes tells of the incredible outreach from some of their friends. "When he found out Michael had been killed, a good friend, two thousand miles away, got in a plane to come be at my side. I also had a business acquaintance who really wasn't that close to me—but apparently he was. He had two boys of his own. He also got on a plane and was down the next day. 'I didn't know what to do, so I did the only thing I could possibly do. That was to come and be with you.' " This is what Allen recommends to anyone who wants to reach out to someone who has lost a child—just be there. "You don't have to do anything. You don't have to say anything. Just your presence counts."

One such friend of Allen and Judith Haimes was Paulette Copia. Paulette had been working in her store. Sensing something was wrong, she suddenly had an impulse to call Judith. Over the telephone she learned from the Haimeses' housekeeper something was indeed wrong. Michael had been in a car accident. Judith and Allen had gone to the hospital with the police officer who came to the house to notify them. Paulette turned to her helper, a young man, and told him she had to leave immediately to go to her friend's home. Her co-worker commented, "If the police have come, it's very bad." But Paulette could not accept that thought in her mind. Driving on the way over to their house, she remembers thinking: I hope Michael is not badly hurt and it doesn't take him a long time to get better.

Upon arriving at the house, Paulette was anxious to know what Michael's condition was. Not wishing to tie up the main phone, she and the housekeeper went upstairs to use the phone in Michael's room to telephone the hospital. Their call was transferred to the emergency room. Dr. Heller, a neighbor of the Haimeses' took the call. He told the housekeeper the sad news. Paulette remembers the housekeeper screamed aloud, "Michael is dead?" Paulette was stupefied. "I was in complete shock. When my own mother died two years earlier, I had felt the impact, and then the crying and mourning, but I never felt the stunned sensation I experienced when I learned Michael had died. I just sat on his bed in a complete daze. I remember looking around his room, just staring at it, trying to realize that Michael was never coming back to it."

Both Karen Tripi and Stephanie Allen lost brothers in car accidents. Karen's friends were sympathetic and listened, but Karen felt they simply could not comprehend the loss she felt. "I had no one to talk to who really understood." Her parents had begun to attend meetings held by The Compassionate Friends, and Karen became active in the organization's siblings' group for surviving brothers and sisters. She relates more easily to the "new friends" who have experienced similar thoughts and emotions. While both Karen and Stephanie were left as the only surviving child, Karen was married. Stephanie was not, although she lived away from home. Stephanie does feel her friends were there up to a point. "I had one very close friend. Our parents knew each other. When my brother died, she was sympathetic. I remember one night coming home from work. My roommate was visiting her parents, and I was alone. I put on all the records, but I was still alone. So I called up this close friend who lived out on the Island and said, 'I just need to come out there,' and she told me to come out."

Karen feels that a lot of people are afraid to talk about the dead person for fear "we will burst into tears and be depressed." No one has to mention her brother's name for Karen to know her brother is dead. She thinks about him much of the time. And she appreciates it when a friend *does* speak her brother's name. Karen feels that in so doing, the friend is stating her brother was cared about and had made an impression on the friend's life in some way, too. "When one of my friends offered to go to the cemetery with me, it made me glad that she cared enough about him to come with me." At the funeral itself Karen was impressed when some of the boys cried. Friends of her brother's came to her parents and said, "We loved him, too." Contrasting with the touching gesture of Billy's friends was the insensitive group of train riders Karen met when returning to work. The group gathered as the train approached, and one rider decided to tell a joke to pass some time. Only the joke was about a dead brother. After he had finished telling it, he suddenly became aware of a silence and realized his blunder. For Karen, he was unthinking and should have realized beforehand the joke would offend her.

In the office Karen fared little better. "After two weeks of everyone's being so nice to me, it was sickening. Everyone treated me completely different from before. No one allowed me to function properly." Karen felt as if she had leprosy. She went into her boss's office and said that if she did something wrong in her work, she wanted to be treated accordingly, like anyone else in the office. Once she said that, it seemed to clear the air. "Things went back to normal." But one day soon after, one of the women in the office had a fight with her brother and passed the comment "Does anyone want a brother?" Karen did! And shook her head in disbelief that this person would be willing to give away something so very precious.

Angela and Peter Purpura tell of their first visit to a meeting at The Compassionate Friends one month after their daughter's death. "It was there over a period of months that we established friendships of a completely different dimension." They met under the worst of circumstances, yet with these complete strangers Angela and Peter could share the most difficult elements of their grief. Here they met people who didn't stand in judgment, with whom they shared the most common denominator. Some they saw only at monthly meetings. With others, they spent their first holidays without their deceased children. They went to cemeteries together, spent anniversaries of their children's death with them, and together learned how to rebuild their lives. "Our surviving children became friends." Over time they learned to laugh and actually have fun together. One man remarked at a meeting that he felt it easier to establish new friends than to hold onto old ones. This echoed Angela's view. Except for a very few, the old friendships were no longer possible for her. There was no going back. With those friends who had children Cassandra's age, Angela couldn't bear to hear how they were growing up, becoming interested in boys, and on and on. "The first meal I was able to prepare was for two Compassionate Friends couples. *They* would understand if the food burned."

Cassandra's best friend was named Eileen. They had grown up together. Eileen's house was the first in which Cassandra had slept overnight. She was the only really close friend Cassandra had to share her dying days. Cassandra and Eileen talked on the phone the few times that Cassandra was hospitalized. When Cassandra was only able to hobble about, Eileen would hold her up. When reading became difficult, Eileen would read to her, join her for meals, play games, and they would talk. No child of ten years could have been more loving, caring, and attentive. The day before Cassandra died, she asked for Eileen. Angela believes it was to say good-bye. Eileen and her family were away camping. Cassandra kept asking for her friend, and Angela kept telephoning, but there was no answer. The family returned too late. Cassandra never had the opportunity to say good-bye to her dear and good friend. A few months later, while Angela was looking through Cassandra's things, she found a small note tucked into a change purse. It read: "Eileen, I love you." It was signed "Cassandra." That night Angela took her younger daughter, Cara, and Eileen out to dinner. Angela offered the note to Eileen. After reading it, Eileen told Angela she could keep it because she had saved in a special box all the notes Cassandra had ever written to her.

Two years later, the Purpuras went to mass on November 29, which would have been Cassandra's eleventh birthday. A touching surprise awaited them. "Our little friend Eileen quietly slipped into the pew beside us. She remembered—as only a special friend could."

Indeed, if only we were all so fortunate as to have a dear and good friend such as Cassandra's Eileen.

Contrasting the friendship Cassandra had with Eileen, we hear the story of another child. The brother of a young boy who had died of cancer suffered bitterly at the hands of friends—both prior to as well as after his brother's death. The boy who died was eight years old. His brother, ten, originally harbored feelings of anger at his brother for being sick and receiving so much attention. Later, when his brother came home during a period of remission, the ten-year-old became the younger boy's protector. Having lost his hair to radiation, the young boy had to wear a hat. Friends would tease him unmercifully in attempts to push his hat off. The boy's brother defended him and later suffered consequences after his brother died. "The kids didn't know how to act. They thought what my brother had was catching, and they wouldn't come near me."

Parents feel adults figuratively say much the same thing.

Once death is so close as happening to their friend's child, that represents their own stark vulnerability. The thought that they, too, might be unable to protect their children from death is unsettling, so much so that although friends may wish to help the bereaved parents, usually they cannot. They are stricken with the dread that the specter of death will appear to them if they are in close proximity—or if they look at the reality of what has happened. The inability of friends to accept the raw pain of such a tragedy often creates among bereaved parents the feeling that friends wish to avoid either seeing them or talking about the death of their child. One parent states, "Perhaps it is not so much that friends do not *wish* to listen as it is that they *cannot* listen. For in listening they hear that they, like we, have no control over safeguarding our children's lives." A defense mechanism then develops, and friends may wish to help the bereaved parent, but not at the risk of exposing their own vulnerability. For the friend, each encounter with the bereaved parent may become a test of hiding these fears. And sometimes they simply cannot be masked.

Often friends have little concept of the incredible strain it is for a newly bereaved parent just to exist. Many friends, having visited or telephoned the grieving parent, believe they should then wait for the parent to call. They are unaware that an anguished parent has no ambition and this type of initiative will be left to the friends, especially in the early months of grieving. As a result, many relationships suffer a little death of their own. To avoid this loss, some bereaved parents have indicated it is often up to the grieving parents to take the initiative to bridge this gap.

Irma Shapiro, whose son, Carl, was killed in an accident, recently wrote a letter to the chapter of The Compassionate Friends whose meetings she attends. "It's many years since we lost our son. I go to The Compassionate Friends. I can't say I go to be comforted. I go because I get a feeling of belonging. In one aspect of my life, a very important one, I'm like all the others there. When everyone has told 'His Story,' the combined hurt is so overwhelming that one has to feel his hurt is less than that with which he came." Irma states she wrote the last part of this letter, which follows below, because of the many people at the meetings "who were quite harsh about nonbereaved parents and some of the insensitive things they said to the bereaved." There were some suggestions that nothing be done precipitously, that parents should hold onto clothes and memorabilia until much time had passed. Irma felt friends and family should be added to the list. "Hold onto them because once you chuck them out, you may not be able to get them back. If you feel sensitive, keep them at arm's length. Tell them you are not ready for relationships now, that you'll be in touch when the pain has passed. Good friends (and that includes family) are hard to come by. What were we like before? Are we special people because we had a loss? Were we special before we had the loss? Did we know how to act, what to say, what not to say—at all times, under all conditions— upon a death, a disability, an illness, an accident or any other catastrophe? Can our child's death serve at least to make us more 'humane,' more tolerant of others in a world that is laden with violence and injustice?"

One parent was reminded of a scene in the classic movie *Never on Sunday* in which actress Melina Mercouri portrayed the role of a Greek prostitute. Her solution to any problem that arose was for everyone to go down to the seashore. While attending a performance of the Greek tragedy *Medea* at the theater with an American friend, Mercouri gives him a knowing smile when the children are murdered. The friend is aghast at her smirk. She quickly explains, "They are not *really* murdered. They are not dead. You will see later." The friend reprimands her, "Of course, they are dead. They have been murdered, killed." But the woman keeps shaking her head in contradiction. At the end of the play, when the cast comes forward to take their bows, out run the little children. "You see."

She smiles. "And now they will all go down to the seashore."

This, then, is perhaps what friends of the bereaved are hoping for—that in the end they will not be forced to accept the realization that a child has died. Friends want to go back to the way it was—they want to go down to the seashore.

For those friends who would wish guidelines in helping the grieving family of a dead child, the following list of "Do's and Don'ts" by Lee Schmidt, R.N., of Parent Bereavement Outreach may prove invaluable.

HELPING BEREAVED PARENTS

Do's and Don'ts

DO'S

—Do let your genuine concern and caring show.

—Do be available . . . to listen, to run errands, to help with the other children, or whatever else seems needed at the time.

—Do say you are sorry about what happened to their child and about their pain.

—Do allow them to express as much grief as they are feeling at the moment and are willing to share.

—Do encourage them to be patient with themselves, not to expect too much of themselves and not to impose any "shoulds" on themselves.

—Do allow them to talk about the child they have lost as much and as often as they want to.

DON'TS

—Don't let your own sense of helplessness keep you from reaching out to a bereaved parent.

—Don't avoid them because you are uncomfortable (being avoided by friends adds pain to an already intolerably painful experience).

—Don't say you know how they feel (unless you've lost a child yourself, you probably don't know how they feel).

—Don't say "you ought to be feeling better by now" or anything else which implies a judgment about their feelings.

—Don't tell them what they *should* feel or do.

—Don't change the subject when they mention their dead child.

DO'S

—Do talk about the special, endearing qualities of the child they've lost.

—Do give special attention to the child's brothers and sisters—at the funeral and in the months to come (they too are hurt and confused and in need of attention which their parents may not be able to give at this time).

—Do reassure them that they did everything that they could, that the medical care their child received was the best or whatever else you know to be *true and positive* about the care given their child.

DONT'S

—Don't avoid mentioning the child's name out of fear of reminding them of their pain (they haven't forgotten it!).

—Don't try to find something positive (e.g., a moral lesson, closer family ties, etc.) about the child's death.

—Don't point out that at least they have their other children (children are not interchangeable; they cannot replace each other).

—Don't say that they can always have another child (even if they wanted to and could, another child would not replace the child they've lost).

—Don't suggest that they should be grateful for their other children (grief over the loss of one child does not discount parents' love and appreciation of their living children).

—Don't make any comments which in any way suggest that the care given their child at home, in the emergency room, hospital, or wherever was inadequate (parents are plagued by feelings of doubt and guilt without any help from their family and friends).

9 · Messages of Hope

Claire and Cliff Kahn's daughter, Donna, died sixteen years ago when she was six and a half years of age. When the baby was two and a half months old, she was diagnosed by the pediatrician as having Niemann-Pick disease—a fatal disease, for which there is no known treatment or cure. The hematologist confirmed the diagnosis, and the young couple were told their baby would probably live only two years or so. "When we learned that our child was dying," Claire says, "we wanted to take care of her at home for as long as we could. For each day was very precious. We were fortunate to be able to care for her at home for her entire life. My husband was very active in caring for our child, and we had tremendous support from our family. There are many pressures on parents who learn their child has a fatal genetic disease; there is the problem of the day-to-day care of their baby and there are questions about having other children."

The Kahns were united in keeping their child at home, whereas sometimes parents have dissenting views. "In some cases of Niemann-Pick and Tay-Sachs children it is much harder. Hospitalization is almost mandated by the twenty-four-hour-a-day nursing care required. There can be tremendous guilt on the parents' part if their child is hospitalized because it appears to be a voluntary action; it is a time often more painful than the actual diagnosis. For a parent of a child with Niemann-Pick disease or Tay-Sachs, the child dies three times: one, at the time the fatal diagnosis is made; two, at hospitalization when the parent no longer can care for the child and separation takes place; and three, at the ultimate death."

Initially Claire and Cliff underwent the overwhelming

shock. "That day becomes italicized in your mind. You remember the weather. You remember everything about that day. When you receive a death sentence, everything changes and nothing changes. Your child is still there for the moment—happy, smiling, yet unbelievably dying. Things happen slowly. And in a way you have time to recoup. I was unable to cope when I would start to think ahead: When she starts having convulsions, what will I do? When she loses her eyesight, how shall I bear it? And when she dies? You learn to step back from that pain and deal with it on a daily basis. You don't cope with the future until you are there. What you don't realize is that by the time you get to those circumstances there has been a period that allows you to deal with them. There are no choices. If you lose your own sanity or well-being, you lose the precious moments of each wonderful day with your child. Indeed, the very thing you value in your child's life and what you wanted for her would be negated."

Claire poignantly describes her feeling about the six-and-a-half years her daughter lived. "You cannot change one day of it for your child, and the overwhelming frustration can be channeled in a positive way. At one year of age Donna leveled off. After eighteen months it was downhill. She was completely blind by that point and did not develop as a normal child. But I got more and more each day out of less and less, until I got absolutely everything out of nothing, for I had the love I could give to my child." Claire tells what happened during subsequent years. "I wanted to give meaning to my child's life. Twenty-two years ago, when Donna was diagnosed, very little was known about rare genetic diseases. Our life took a positive expression in our work with the National Tay-Sachs and Allied Diseases Foundation. In dealing with the diagnosis and the day-to-day care of their child, it becomes vitally important for parents to be in touch with other parents who have gone through this and who want to share their experiences. My first reaction when I heard about the organization was that I didn't need group therapy. We went out of curiosity. What we found were people like ourselves who were not wringing their hands in despair. We found parents who wanted to help take away the isolation these diseases presented to other parents. We found parents who wanted to change the picture so that something so cataclysmic in our lives—our child's brief twilight existence—could have meaning. And one day perhaps—through research—another child and another parent can be spared this pain."

Six months after her son died, Judith Haimes decided to give a shower for a friend who was pregnant. The reason Judith wanted to do this, aside from the fact her friend was going to have a baby, was that she had a goal. She wanted all her friends to gather together. She wanted all those who had been worried about her to see that she was coming back to the world of the living. "All my friends were walking around on eggshells, and I had given them plenty of reason to do so. I had shut myself off from them in a lot of ways." Judith wanted her friends to be with her once again, to laugh together, and to see that she was able to have fun. And now, when she sees her friends, for however brief a moment, it's not like sitting around in a tomb. "They realize now that since I can laugh, it's okay for them to laugh, and it's not irreverent." Judith believes that people want to help and touch and take the pain away, but they don't know how. "And unless the person who has lost someone shows them how, they will never be able to do it. It's not fair to make other people pay forever because you are having grief in your life."

Judith says that in surviving, you can't do everything as you once did. "Everyone has a thing they can't do—like going to the cemetery, or back to a favorite spot of your child's, or to a supermarket where your child may have shopped with you, or to any place that stirs painful memories. Although you will go forward in many areas, there are also many areas in which you cannot go back." Judith believes that ten years from now certain things will always bother a bereaved parent, whether it is not being able to go to a graduation or birthday of a child's friend or any number of things. "In recovering, you can't do everything as you once did, but that does not mean you are not recovering.

"Each of us, being mortal, will have hang-ups that affect our daily lives. For the happy memories of activities shared with a child can be as agonizing to endure as sad ones. And if going to a store where your child was exuberant, bouncing with energy and running about, reminds you of times too painful to bear, you simply cannot go back. For each of us, there is a place we cannot return to, lest those bittersweet memories take too great a toll. Not only do parents live with the not-going-back issue, but they must also deal with daily events that often create havoc months, years after the death of their child." Judith cites an example. "Yesterday I freaked out. I heard an ambulance. I looked at the clock. It was four-forty, the same time Michael had died. I thought, Oh, dear God, and it all came rushing back to me. At just that moment my husband telephoned and asked if I was all right. I told him I had been having a really rough moment, but I was all right now that he had called."

Judith says parents go through periods when they think they are going to die, but they come out of it. "But when you come out of it, you don't go lie on the bed retching and vomiting. You finish ironing, or you finish pushing a child on a swing, or you finish feeding the baby." Judith began to deal with her pain. "There comes a point when every parent says, 'How can I deal with this?' and when you just have to say, 'My husband's pain and well-being are more important than what I am feeling, and if I have to fake it to get through today and put a smile on my face, then, by God, I'm going to fake it because all my tears aren't going to bring back my child. But all my tears may drive my other children away, may hurt my husband more.' There comes a time when you must stop putting yourself and your pain first."

Judith feels it is time for her to start helping her children with their grief as they have been helping with hers. She has seen many siblings stand tall in their brave efforts to help their parents. "When my children see their mother start to fall apart, then their foundation is wrecked. And that is why they work very hard. Aside from the love and the caring, they work hard because when their foundation gets wrecked, they are going to fall apart, and they are going to lose control. It's now time for them to see that we all will miss Michael and we all will love him, and we will never get over his death. But we all have each other, and it is okay for us to cry together. It is okay for us to miss him together. But they no longer have to fight to help keep Mom and Dad sane.

"If parents have some set goal, if they can help someone else, if they can become involved, they can survive. For the survivors, the key is to put other people ahead of themselves." Judith Haimes believes very strongly that her priorities have changed, her values have changed, she has changed. "I am not the same person. I am fighting very hard for the survival of my being. I want to make things good again for my husband and children. I don't want to see that terrible pain in Allen's eyes when he looks at me because he sees how I am suffering. For every mother and every father in the entire world who has ever lost a child, ask any of them. It never goes away. But you can pull together or you can pull apart."

Judith encourages parents to seek the positive rather than the negative way to survive. "This lingering grief is not something where you wake up one day and say the pain is gone. This survival is like that of an alcoholic. You take it one day at a time. You survive one day at a time. And that goes on until you draw your last breath. There is never a day that goes by when you won't think of your child. There is never a day that goes by when you won't have pain. It's just that you are much more in control of it. It is still there. The pain is still real, but you can survive the pain. You can survive the hard way, or you can survive the easy way. Either way you are going to continue living. In reality there is no easy way, but there is an easier way than staying negative.

"There is absolutely nothing that can be done to bring back our child. Nothing. If there was, we would be doing it, all of us. We would sell our souls to Beelzebub if necessary. But there is no way we can bring back that child. Since there is nothing we can do to change that, we have to get on with living; either that or just go ahead and die. But if you stay negative, not only are you dying, but you are decaying. You are infecting everything and everyone around you. The scars you are giving the people who truly love you they will never overcome. There will come a time when they can survive the death of this child, but will they ever be able to survive the scars they incurred along the way?"

Judith does not feel it is her place to judge how any mother or father feels when they have lost a child. "It's just that the pain of some parents is so severe it eats them alive like a cancer. There has to be a way someone can talk to them and show them that the pain is not going to stop and that their beautiful child is not going to take one extra breath. Nothing is going to change what happened. But put the pain in a little place in the back of your mind where you can deal with it, and go on. Stop hurting everyone around you."

In coping with the question of *why?* Judith comments, "It doesn't matter why. Even if we had the answer, it wouldn't change anything. People have to go on living for those around them, those they love. It's almost like saying, 'For once in your life, muster up all the strength you possibly can. Be the Don Quixote when you have nothing else to give. Put yourself aside, and put other people ahead of you.' Again, it is not fair to judge another parent. I, of all people, know the pain a parent goes through. But realize that you have to continue living or you just die. And if you are going to die, then go die, but don't take everybody with you. If you have a contagious disease, then go someplace the way Typhoid Mary did and be imprisoned the rest of your life and suffer alone. Don't infect everyone you come in contact with."

In describing how parents are affected prior to and after the first anniversary of the death of their child, Judith comments: "In these agonizing twelve months, every now and then that disgustingly sickening feeling hits you in the pit of your stomach where you think you are going to vomit, when you start to relive everything that happened. But, the nineteenth really was not any different from any other day as far as missing Michael. I have talked to other people who have said this anniversary date is so anticlimactic because you wait for it, you know it's coming, and then when it gets there—nothing. I believe that the day after the anniversary was worse, because on that day we said, 'My God, it's been over a year. Can you believe Michael's been dead over a year?' The first year, when the pain can kill you, when it eats you alive like the most rampant cancer, every time it starts to come near you, you cringe. You can not bear to relive it. But, after a year, you can look at it, and feel it, but you are not dying with it. And, it is a terrible pain, but you know that after you relive this whole experience, you will be okay." Judith feels by the time parents get to the second year, they realize they are still alive and still doing all the things that have to be done. "They realize that next year it will be two years since that child died. And, though there is not a day that goes by that you don't think about that child, now when you think about him, it's about the good as well as the bad. You just don't think, 'My God, he's dead.' You remember the way he came home from school, the things he liked, his favorite meal.

"Nothing changes after one year and everything changes. After that year the pain is just as acute as it always was, but you know how to control it. You know how to survive and control that pain the same as if your legs have been cut off, you know they will never grow back. Yesterday, I cleaned out my bookshelf and came across a lot of Michael's books. And, sure it hurt. But Michael's not coming back for them. I *know* he is not coming back for them. There is that reality. But I have survived that first year! And if you get through that intact, then you have a fighting chance to hold on and continue."

Judith urges parents not to feel afraid or guilty in terms of the word *recovering*. "Just because parents can't do certain things, they shouldn't think that precludes recovery. There will always be memories a parent cannot face. Years from now certain things will still bother you, whether it is not being able to go to the graduation of your child's friend or going back to a seaside resort where your child laughed and went swimming. Sure, there will always be some bad memories, but that doesn't mean you are not recovering. And getting on with living doesn't mean a parent has to feel disloyal to his child's memory. *To recover doesn't mean you have to forget. You will always remember. So why not remember the good things in your child's life?"*

After her son's suicide Leonora Hollander had thoughts of suicide, too. She couldn't talk to people. She was hiding from everyone. She was afraid of going out and became a prisoner in her own home. Unable to face passing by her son's room, she moved to a new apartment. This required calling a carpenter, looking for carpeting, and many other details attendant in moving. "I went through the motions, but I had no feeling. I was like a zombie. I was cold. It just wasn't me. I went back to work, but I wasn't functioning. When people would come in and say something to me, I would lose control. I couldn't look at young boys walking by on the street with T-shirts and jeans or boys playing in the park or riding a bike. I couldn't stand being in the supermarket."

For the first year after her son's death Leonora was continuously ill. She simply wanted to go to bed at night and not get up in the morning. "I knew I had to get help. After some inquiries, I was sent to Dr. Roberta Temes, a grief counselor. Dr. Temes saved my life. She helped explain feelings and thoughts, and she helped me become active again. If it were not for her, I surely would be in the grave next to my son." From time to time Leonora still has nightmares, but she has been able to return to the mainstream of life. She cares for an elderly mother. She works. She visits with friends and neighbors. She has made friends with a young family near her and has a warm relationship with their children. The youngsters and Leonora exchange gifts and sentiments, and it is a happiness to her to have found friends. She is active in sports. She cooks, crochets hats for various individuals, and on the whole is able to say, "I guess God gave me the strength to survive. I guess I am a fighter."

Doris Young, whose eight-year-old son drowned, also had nightmares. But some months after his death she had another type of dream—"you might say it was a vision, almost." Doris felt she was not fully asleep one afternoon while lying on the sofa. She could hear everything outside and could hear the television. Suddenly her son appeared before her, but not as a little boy anymore. "It was Irvin, but he was like a teenager. He said, 'Mom, I'm all right.' It was so clear to me, and he had such a happy expression on his face. I had had it in my mind for so long that my boy had screamed for help and no one had been there. I always pictured that he was calling for help. But here I saw a smile on his face. And it took a great weight off me, almost as if he himself were telling me not to feel this way." Doris felt that with all the other help she had received this vision of her son was the one thing that lifted the heavy burden of guilt she had carried. "I know he came to me. It was really and truly the kind of relief I needed from the anguish of wondering how he died. I know some people will say I imagined it, or I was crazy. I really can't explain it, but I *know* it was real."

Frances Groden, age ninety-one at this writing, is an incredible example of courage and fortitude. When we think in terms of losing a child, often we think in terms of a teenager. It does not matter what the age of a child, it will always be a child to the parent. And no matter what age your child may be, when your child has died, it affects you forever. Frances's daughter, Goldie, developed cancer of the hip and died when she was thirty-nine years old. Even now, twenty years later, Frances tries to fill the void. She felt she wanted to do something and be useful in life. "I didn't want simply to sit on my rear end." She began to do volunteer work at the community hospital nearby, working in any capacity that would be helpful, whether stuffing envelopes for mailings or whatever. "It took me away from the house. I didn't have to look at the four walls. More important, I served a purpose."

The words *I served a purpose* were the mainstay for Frances in helping her surmount waves of grief and loneliness. In her desire to comfort and aid others, Frances urges parents to get themselves out of the house. "Even if you feel your worst, do something—anything. Sort out clothes in the closet, sweep the floor, vacuum the rug. Most important of all, push yourself out of the house. Walk just one block if that's all you can manage, but walk it. If it helps, count the lines on the sidewalk blocks or anything that will allow you a brief period of thinking of something other than your grief." Frances later joined a senior citizens' group. One day flu injections were being given to the group. In order to maintain order—the group was quite talkative—one of the health volunteers began showing them how to do calisthenics while sitting down. Frances found the young woman volunteer so charming in manner she asked her a question: "May I adopt you?" The young lady responded,

"How would you like to be adopted? Would you like to be a Brownie grandmother?" Frances was elated. "I never envied anyone or was jealous of anyone. But I often used to think at a wedding: 'Why couldn't that be my daughter?' I would yearn for grandchildren I would never have." And now she was a Brownie grandmother. What a marvelous "sharing" she was able to enjoy. Frances Groden was able to offer her adopted grandchildren far more than any monetary contribution—she was able to offer herself. "Grandma Groden" was *there* for many young Brownies—to listen about their joys and their sorrows, to help when she was needed.

Sue Matthews lost her baby daughter when the child was only seven days old. She reflects on her attempts to survive the loss of her baby. "Watching or observing oneself recover from grief is much like watching a child grow. No measurements are taken daily, but all of a sudden the child's jeans are too short, and one is sure the child is growing. In the same respect, as I recover from my grief, there are some leaps that seemed to have taken place, yet they were probably not one-day leaps— they were two- or three-month leaps." After entering a painful period of *why?* Sue decided to busy herself with as many activities as possible. She began to escort a small group of five-year-olds to the movies, take them skating, etc. She took two difficult graduate classes and threw herself into them. "I felt I wouldn't have time to see her sweet little face." But she began to experience insomnia and was frightened she was pregnant again. This "suspected" pregnancy had a devastating effect on Sue. "Midterms were approaching eleven weeks after her death. It was also then I met Elizabeth's due date (she had been premature). And it was my mother's birthday as well. Probably most of these factors together sent me into a frightening maelstrom." Her severe insomnia also alarmed her. "I had attended two SHARE meetings at this point but had not been able to say the words *My baby died* publicly. It was comforting to know I wasn't alone. However, it wasn't SHARE alone that saved me—I believe it was God and my new specialist. A lot of people were praying for me at that time, and I've seen the power of prayer."

One of the most important questions for Sue still remained: Why? For what possible reason was her child taken from her? "I truly believe this question must be at least partially resolved in order to survive. I am not a charismatic Christian, and I try to be very careful about what our minister classifies as the warm fuzzies, which people describe as religious experiences. But one morning I was driving to school, and I remember crying out to God, 'Why have you taken all the joy out of my life?' And an answer echoed back: 'That you may know how sweet life is.' It was not *my* answer. But I remember thinking then that was His answer for that time."

The "real leap" came for Sue approximately six months later. Her minister asked her to go talk to a young mother who had lost her first child a few days before. She did. Four and a half hours later she left the young woman's apartment feeling much stronger herself. "I felt strangely comforted, yet knowing that I had given her much comfort and understanding. It was then I truly realized my loss was 'not for nothing.' Elizabeth's death was not in vain. If I had to capsulize my philosophy of recovering, it would be to make the loss count—make it meaningful. But it should be stressed that helping others cannot be done until the individual experiencing the loss has at least partially resolved his or her own grief. This does take some time. Because of my suffering and my comfort, I was then able to give comfort. That is enough of an answer for me. God had revealed 'just enough'—not everything—but just enough for me. I would urge parents to read Corinthians one:three-seven. This passage has been so meaningful. And now the young mother I helped, Luanne, is helping others in her SHARE chapter in Champaign."

Ernie Freireich, whose son, Mark, died after being in a coma for four months following a car accident in 1975, believes bereaved parents who permit themselves to grieve genuinely will experience some guilt and self-recrimination. "Probably no other single factor in the arsenal of bereavement is more debilitating than unresolved and excessive guilt." Ernie gives his thoughts on bereavement and guilt:

Guilt, when left to smolder in our minds, can destroy the joy of living, endanger our marriages, and humiliate us to the point of suicide. It can become the underlying cause of emotional illness, constant fatigue, and the self-punishing conditions of frigidity and drug addiction.

Bereaved parents come to feel there was something we should have done and did not, or something we may have done and should not have. We act as judge and jury and almost always end up "guilty as charged."

We are always saying to ourselves, "I really should have . . ." and, "I should have delayed or put it off," and "Well, I guess it is too late now." "If only . . ." becomes a substitute verbiage for the reality of "Why didn't I tell him then how much I loved him!" or "Why did I have to quarrel with him before he left?" or "Why didn't I buy that certain something she wanted so badly?" We persecute ourselves for having failed our children in a multitude of ways.

All parents regret failing to have done something that could have prevented the death. The implication is that we see ourselves in control of our destiny as well as the destiny of others. There is no logic in our thinking that we were in possession of some godlike power to prevent what happened.

Many times we accuse ourselves of negligence. The death of our child deprives us of our competency as parents. At least we look upon it in that way. Our feelings of guilt are often borne out of those things we could have or should have done and did not.

Doesn't the loving parent keep from giving his children everything as an object lesson of real life? Weren't we trying to pass on to them a sense of right and wrong, values to live by . . . our values? Didn't we do these things because never in our worst imaginings did we think there would be no tomorrow for them?

We must come to understand that bereavement and guilt go hand in hand. Our circumstances of guilt are reinforced by our feelings of helplessness because we were powerless to alter the circumstances. There is nothing we can do now because it is too late. Our guilt is very often the basic reason why it is difficult to return to that so-called state of normalcy and get on with the daily business of living.

We refuse to accept the helplessness that was afforded us, even though the circumstances were unavoidable. We come to believe that somehow we could have changed the outcome and didn't.

But let us think about it. Isn't it perfectly normal for me to feel guilty? Isn't that one of the consequences of being a loving and sensitive parent?

Do not bury or deny your feelings of guilt. Deal with them. Seek the reasons for the way you feel. Ask yourself if you really should feel guilty. Are you hiding a secret feeling of guilt that you can share with someone else?

Our sense of self-worth and the intensity of our guilt vary from person to person. Do what is right for you. Remember, perfection is an unattainable concept. Mistakes can, will, and must happen. Coming to terms with one's guilt is emotionally healthier than living in endless misery.

Yes, there are regrets, and because we are human, there will always be regrets. They teach us to strive for a more meaningful and loving relationship with those with whom we live and share.

Dr. Peter Purpura, the bereaved father who is also a clinical psychologist, tells of some pitfalls to look for in surviving the death of a child. "The work that has to be done in mourning is not understanding *why* the child has died. If one gets caught up in the *why?*, it is a way of avoiding the fact that the child has died. You must come to terms with the issue—that your child is dead. By accepting the *that*, you deal with the *why?* Some never know why on a physical basis, some never know why on a circumstantial basis, and some never know why on a cosmic basis. It becomes a question of having to put the *why?* aside and come to the reality that children die. It is not a question of *why* they do; they just do. The real issue is the reality *that* the child has died. This has to be accepted. We will never really understand." Peter also cautions parents about getting well *too soon*. "Strange as it may sound, there can be problems with getting well too quickly. It's like the scab on a wound that may heal on top but inside is still festering. Many times what appears on the surface to be a parent getting well amazingly fast will often emerge later in tragic ways."

Fred Wiener, whose daughter Frances, age thirty-one, was killed in a car crash in 1980, tells of such an incident. "I was fortunate enough to be able to cry—to be able to let it out the way I did. A woman I knew in business had a son who committed suicide. The husband couldn't let it out. He seemed to be functioning well and returned to business and was doing all right. But later he had a nervous breakdown and had to be hospitalized." In dealing with his own grief, Fred joined the Knights of Pythias to do something different from the normal pattern of things—to make a change. His wife, Edith, had always been active in local hospital work. After a time she began to become active in the hospital's fund-raising efforts. "You force yourself to keep going. After about a year we went to our first movie. Then we began to go a little more often. We again started playing cards, which we hadn't done in a long time." Edith had always wanted to move to Florida. Instead, Fred convinced her to buy a condominium, not as a pleasure place, but as a retreat. "That is what we did, and it is one of the smartest things we could have done. We are like new people for the while we are there. It is a change, and it helps."

Abe Malawski reflects on his feelings after the first anniversary of his son's death: "In looking back on how we managed to live through a whole year, it's amazing we made it in one piece. I think I shed a thousand tears. I think I cried on a lot of shoulders. And I think I taught my friends how they should treat a bereaved parent—that we don't have a disease and we like to talk about Harvey, our Harvey. He existed for nearly twenty years and just because he is no longer with us now that he is dead, he hasn't stopped being with us. I think we have grown taller. We have grown more caring. Judy and I have gotten closer. Our son, Steven, has become more meaningful. Our bereavement friends have become special to us. What I am trying to say to someone who just lost a child is, they will hear everyone saying, 'Time, time will help you.' And they don't believe it. I know I didn't believe it, but it works—oh, yes, it works. There have been many days when just going through minute after minute was impossible. There were days I was so depressed and so far down, I couldn't go any lower. I had to be going up. I have told Judy I care and that I love her. And, she has told me the same thing. Steven has gotten more caring and is aware of the fact that he needs us as much as we need him. I never thought we could grow so much in a year."

Abe stresses that you never forget your child. "We have not forgotten Harvey, for that is impossible. But, at times, I was able to help other bereaved friends when they called on the phone to say, 'I feel lousy and I am hurting.' And I was able to spew forth thoughts and words without knowing what I was saying. But, the fact they told me I helped them made me feel very, very good. So I guess there is a strength in all of us that we can comfort someone in the same circumstances." Abe and Judy discovered just how important that sharing was when they spent the anniversary of their son's death with another bereaved couple. "Two days ago was Harvey's first anniversary. We went to the cemetery. Judy had told me a week before she didn't want to come back home from the cemetery because she felt it was going to be very difficult. I told her we would come up with something to do. Unbeknownst to me she called one of the couples that we go to group therapy with and they invited us to come to their house after the cemetery. Until Sunday came, it was almost impossible to bear. I had an easier week than Judy. She kept on falling down and getting up through the whole week. She stumbled more than she walked. On Sunday, we went to the cemetery and we managed to get through that mainly by being there. Afterward, we went to be with our friends. We sat around and had coffee and cake. We talked about their son and we talked about Harvey. Then, they asked us to eat out with them. Believe it or not, those four or five hours we spent together enabled us to talk and cry and laugh—and not be afraid of laughing or crying, depending on the circumstances of what we were discussing. I am sure that others there looking at us thought we were four nuts, laughing and crying at the same time."

Abe feels the amount of help you get from someone who has lost a child is immeasurable when you are feeling "down." And he describes his outlook for the future: "We survived a year. I expect to survive next year and however many more years I have left. That doesn't mean it was an easy year, but don't let's say it was not positive. Because it was. The mere fact that we survived it shows how positive it has been. And, to anyone calling out to me and crying to me and saying to me, 'I am drowning,' I would like to think I can help—any time, any day, any hour—just by trying to tell them, 'Well, I made it, didn't I!' "

As has been stressed throughout by other parents, it is not the *amount* of time, but *how* that time is utilized. Abe and Judy Malawski were able to recognize that attending a meeting at a peer group once a month was not enough. They sought further help and have been going to group therapy sessions weekly. Unless the initiative is taken by the parents to seek help, that magical word "time" doesn't exist. Abe and Judy had a choice. They made the decision to help themselves—not only in seeking help through the peer organization or group therapy, but in recognizing their need to reach out to other bereaved parents.

Anne Frank was only one of 100,000 Dutch Jews annihilated in the Holocaust. Up to that time she had attended the grammar school in Amsterdam for six years. While the Dutch were aware that bad things were taking place, they could not accept the reality. "This can't be happening to us." Like so many of us facing incomprehensible and devastating news, we feel it only happens to other people. But any child you see in a schoolroom today could have been Anne Frank.

On June 12, 1942, Anne's thirteenth birthday, her father, Otto Frank, stopped at a bookshop to buy her a birthday present. He purchased something a young girl would appreciate— an album in which to keep a diary. Anne was elated and wrote in it right away. Little did she or her father dream that the diary—which poignantly details Anne's innermost thoughts during the two-year period she and her family hid from the Nazis—would remain to speak for her, indeed, speak for all those who believed cruelties in the world must be uprooted. Anne's writings convey the strong feeling that good will ultimately conquer all.

The cherished ideals of a young girl who believed in the inner goodness of man were to be a great comfort to Otto Frank later. He was near death when Russian troops liberated Auschwitz in 1945. Eventually, after realizing all his family were dead, he discovered that a friend had retrieved Anne's diary from a hiding spot. Otto Frank died in 1980 at the age of ninety-one. A recent television program, "The Eternal Light," presented by NBC, showed that the last thirty years of his life were devoted to building for the future, especially for the young. Anne's diary was published initially in 1946, with

1,000 copies. Today more than 15 million copies have been sold, with translations into fifty-six languages.

The spirit and hope of Anne's deep and serious thoughts captured the minds and hearts of millions of youngsters, who wrote to Otto Frank, asking him questions. Otto Frank commented that he was not a bitter man and felt he could aid other children, particularly in adolescence, to gain confidence and hope for their own lives through reading about Anne and her experiences. By encouraging all children of the world to send their questions to him, this bereaved father, whose child died in such a tragic period of history, was able to grant them the same gift he had given to his own daughter—a way of expressing their innermost thoughts in the hope that good will come in the world.

And so it is with the bereaved families in this book who have told of their struggles to live—a day at a time. They, too, have expressed their innermost thoughts in the hope their experiences may benefit others.

Part Two

Helping Hands

Recovering doesn't mean you have to forget.

If you find you are unable to find a way to help yourself, write to me at the address shown below. I will do my utmost to put you in touch with parents who may have found a solution to the problems you have encountered. The message of this book is to offer hope—to know there is indeed a light at the end of the tunnel. It is there, and you can find it. You can survive—if you choose to survive.

Katherine Fair Donnelly, Author
c/o Macmillan Publishing Company
866 Third Avenue
New York, New York 10022

10 · Descriptions of Organizations that Help Bereaved Families

There is a story about two friends who met for lunch one day. Each had been to see doctors concerning ailments. One woman had gone to see Dr. Brown and was told in an abrupt manner she needed to have a hysterectomy. The doctor was extremely brusque. He said there was no question about it and urged her to have this done as soon as possible. The woman didn't like the attitude of the doctor. She didn't like his manner and felt she was being rushed into surgery. So she went to see Dr. Green. His tone was completely different. Soft-spoken in voice, he told the woman, "You poor dear, you must feel very uncomfortable. Well, it's possible we may have to perform a hysterectomy, but let's wait a little while and see." The woman was reassured and felt more comfortable after talking to Dr. Green. Now she was anxious to tell her friend about the visits to the two doctors and how happy she was she had gone to Dr. Green. But when the two women met, her friend told her story first. It seems she had gone to see a Dr. Brown—the same Dr. Brown—and she began to rave about how wonderful he was. "He was so straightforward in his approach. He didn't beat around the bush. He told me exactly what was wrong, and I appreciated his directness." Then the friend related how upset she had been because she had gone to see a Dr. Green. "All he wanted to do was hold my hand and say, 'Oh, you poor dear.'"

What works best for one person may not suit another. After the loss of a child, there are no rights and no wrongs as to what is good for each bereaved family. It is right if you are comfortable. It is wrong if you are uncomfortable. But what is right for someone else is not necessarily the thing that is right for you. And so we arrive at this question: Where can bereaved parents and surviving children find help for the terrible loss they have experienced, for the devastating pain that the death of a child has brought to their lives?

Helping hands come in many forms—through mutual support groups, individual or group therapy, religion, and "bibliotherapy" with listings of books to read. Since each family is different and each person is different, no one helping hand is the right one for everybody—but there are many helping hands! And all share the common goal of wanting to help hurting bereaved families. As one parent described it, "There are different strokes for different folks." While this may sound facetious and somewhat flip, it conveys the point that *there are no rights and no wrongs* here. If it is good for you, then it is right. If it isn't, make a change! Try another way.

For example, some people may like a Chevrolet car, others may prefer a Ford; still others, a foreign car. Although they all may get to the same place, some people are more comfortable with one means than another. So it is with bereaved parents and surviving children. Some may be more at ease in a group setting; others may not. Some may find organizations extremely helpful, while others may find it is simply not for them. Some may prefer the intimate setting of a family doctor's office, their clergyman, or a counselor and may have a very good experience. Others may have an absolutely rotten experience and may have to look further.

It is urgent for bereaved families to realize that there *are* alternatives. There are other helping hands. If you tried the Chevrolet and it wasn't right for you, then check out the other cars. Find one that feels comfortable to you—because that way is the *right* way for you. If you were not happy when you tried the first car, don't despair that there is no other way. If you are made to feel uncomfortable, make a change! There *are* other ways. You will find one that is right for you.

Some of those ways are indicated in this section of the book. There are organizations that offer understanding and caring.

Descriptions of these will be given in detail. Many of the self-help groups also provide programs to assist surviving siblings in their grief. Younger children in bereaved families are often helped by teachers in school who are finding ways of talking about death. Working with children of all ages are the counselors and therapists who also help parents in need of working out their grief. The compassion of a family doctor or community clergyman can be of help after the loss of a child. There are also many helpful books available for parents who prefer to read. A list of suggested reading appears at the back of this book.

Following is an alphabetical listing of organizations that help bereaved families, with descriptions of their activities and programs. A directory of organizations, with information on local chapters, may be found in Chapter 11.

AMERICAN ASSOCIATION FOR MARRIAGE AND FAMILY THERAPY, INC.

We know that people need to go through periods of grieving until they are able to accept what is unalterable. Much of how people react to tragedies has to do with what they experienced early in life in their family of origin and how they saw other family members deal with loss. We are basically an association of well-trained individual therapists who specialize in all phases of marriage and family life. In the course of our work with individuals, couples, and families we often have to help people deal with illness and death of family members and for this reason have experience and knowledge in how to be of help.

In my practice I found that often siblings who experienced

the loss of a brother or sister and who lived with parents steeped in their grief try desperately to replace this child for their parents and have later identity problems. They feel they can never live up to what parents feel the lost child would have been. Parents often become overprotective and hamper the other children's need for independence. So such families should be encouraged to seek help for all members concerned.

Dr. Ruth Neubauer, president of the New York Association for Marriage and Family Therapy, in her statement above indicates some of the areas their organization helps bereaved families. "Losing a child often puts marriage to its severest test, and it is wise for such couples to seek individual and marital help." Dr. Neubauer also believes group therapy is of much help to couples who have gone through the loss of a child.

The American Association for Marriage and Family Therapy is the professional organization for marriage and family therapists. More than 8,000 members throughout the United States and Canada include persons trained in psychology, marriage and family therapy, psychiatry, pastoral counseling, and social work—all of whom are highly trained professional therapists working to help couples solve their marriage and family problems.

The AAMFT carries on intensive educational programs to help people understand more about marriage and family problems, the role of counseling in preventing and solving these problems, as well as the dangers of unscrupulous or unqualified persons who pose as marriage and family therapists. For the public the AAMFT provides a nationwide referral service by supplying the names of qualified marriage and family therapists and general guidelines for seeking their help. A listing by state of the subdivisions of the AAMFT appears at the end of this book. However, to obtain most current information, it is best to write to their national office at:

American Association for Marriage and Family Therapy
1717 K Street, N.W. Suite 407
Washington, D.C. 20006
Telephone: (202) 429-1825

This telephone is toll-free. Information can be obtained about the area in which you live.

The staff and members of the AAMFT provide material on marriage and family problems to various citizen groups, to radio and television broadcasters, newspapers, and magazines, and they also write extensively for professional journals. The association publishes its own journal, *The Journal of Marital and Family Therapy.*

CANDLELIGHTERS AND
THE CANDLELIGHTERS FOUNDATION

Candlelighters is an international organization of parent groups who have or have had children with cancer. Some groups have youth auxiliaries for teenage cancer patients and for teenage siblings of cancer.

The group provides guidance in coping with cancer's effects on parents and on the family and seeks to ease frustrations and fears through the sharing of common experiences.

Candlelighters includes more than 155 chapters, affiliated parent groups and contacts in the United States, Australia, Belgium, Brazil, Canada, Chile, Denmark, England, France, Guatemala, Germany, Indonesia, Mexico, New Zealand, South Africa, and the West Indies. It is a nonprofit organization with emphasis on promoting an emotional support system of "second families" to each other, as well as identifying patient and family needs so that medical and social systems respond adequately.

Groups sponsor twenty-four-hour crisis lines, buddy systems, parent-to-parent contact, professional counseling, and self-help groups. Candlelighters also holds social functions where families can meet and relax in a supportive nonthreatening setting. "Candlelighters cares in the unique way only parents of other child cancer patients can."

The Candlelighters Foundation is the coordinator and educational arm of the parents' groups. It helps new groups to form, acts as liaison to existing groups, and offers communication services. The free services and publications are supported through tax-exempt donations and a grant from the American Cancer Society, Inc. Should you wish further information, please write to:

The Candlelighters Foundation
Suite 1011
2025 Eye Street, NW
Washington, D.C. 20006
Telephone: (202) 659-5136

CENTERS FOR ATTITUDINAL RESEARCH

The Center for Attitudinal Research in Tiburon, California, is a nonprofit, nonsectarian group, originated largely through the efforts of child psychiatrist Gerald Jampolsky, M.D. Programs initially were established for children with life-threatening or catastrophic illnesses. Traditional health care is supplemented by providing an environment in which the children can actively participate. For a child experiencing a catastrophic illness, there is a temptation to feel anger toward the world, a sense of being different and alone. Dr. Jampolsky and the staff at the center strive to ease these stressful tensions.

The Young Children's Group directs its attention to children aged six to sixteen and offers a sharing, loving, supportive program with the use of art and music. Similarly, siblings of children with life-threatening illnesses need to share their fears and anxieties, their feelings of loneliness and unhappiness. Often they feel less loved then the brother or sister being given so much attention by their parents. In the siblings' group, common fears, anger, and guilt feelings about sick or dying brothers and sisters are discussed in a supportive atmosphere. A phone pal/pen pal program has been established whereby children, their siblings, and their parents can relate via phone or letter with people who have had similar life experiences.

The parents' groups at the center provide opportunities to share the concerns and fears families must face during the trauma of life-threatening illness and to provide support for one another. Mothers and fathers often wish to talk to other parents facing a similar crisis with children beset by catastrophic illness. Parents who are faced with the final realization that their child is gone are able to talk to other parents who have endured such sorrow. In one such telephone meeting a newly bereaved parent who had contemplated suicide after the death of his child asked the parents at the other end of the phone, "How did you survive?" Their answer was: "We really don't know how we did. But we are here talking to you, so you know that we did. And we want you to know we understand. We care, and we are here to help you." Just the realization that someone else had experienced his pain, his sorrow, gave this grief-stricken father something to hold onto.

Offshoots of the Center for Attitudinal Research are being established throughout the country. Incredibly all the programs at the center are provided free of charge. The center participates in workshops locally and nationally and offers assistance to those wishing to start other centers. Should you desire further information, contact:

The Center for Attitudinal Healing
19 Main Street
Tiburon, California 94920
Telephone: (415) 435-5022

THE COMPASSIONATE FRIENDS, INC.

This voluntary self-help organization offers understanding and the hand of friendship to bereaved parents. Its main purpose is to assist parents in the positive resolution of the grief they experience after the death of their child. Further, it promotes the physical and emotional health of bereaved parents and surviving children.

At meetings of The Compassionate Friends, parents who have endured the anguish of losing a child offer caring support. They help bereaved parents cope with the grief reactions after the loss of a child, such as disbelief, anger, guilt, despair, loneliness, fear, and personal loss. The organization charges no dues and has no religious affiliation. Some parents come once or twice, and others come over a longer period. Still others continue with the purpose of offering support to newly bereaved parents.

A bereaved parent contacting the main office indicated below will be responded to individually and whenever possible will also be referred to the name, address, and phone of the closest local chapter leader. At the end of this book is a Directory of Helping Organizations, in which there is a listing of the cities which have chapters of The Compassionate Friends, with more being added daily as a result of the rapid expansion of this dedicated organization. Its goal is to lighten the burden of grief for bereaved parents.

Because of the changes that take place in telephone numbers and addresses and to insure a bereaved parent of the latest and most accurate referral information, in their area, all inquires are to be directed to:

The Compassionate Friends, Inc.
National Headquarters
P.O. Box 1347
Oak Brook, Illinois 60521

Should any additional information be desired, a volunteer is available weekdays from 10:00 A.M. to 3:00 P.M. CST at the following telephone number and would be glad to speak to you: (312) 323-5010

The Compassionate Friends was established in Coventry,

England, in 1969, by the assistant to the chaplain in the Coventry and Warwickshire Hospital, the Reverend Mr. Simon Stephens. Each year, because of illness and accidents, many children died in the hospital. After the deaths of two young boys there the parents of the children met by chance, and their grief was lessened by their mutual grieving—by listening to each other, by crying together, by understanding how each felt. These two couples, together with other bereaved parents, asked the Reverend Mr. Stephens to work with them, resulting in an organization offering friendship, understanding, care, and support to other bereaved parents. The organization grew throughout England and later spread to the United States. Since then almost 300 chapters have been established throughout the United States. There are also chapters in England, Australia, and Canada. The aims of a chapter are:

To offer support and friendship to any sorrowing parent, regardless of race, creed or financial status.

To listen with understanding and provide "telephone friends" who may be called.

To provide sharing groups that meet monthly.

To give cognitive information about the grieving process through programs and library.

To provide acquaintance with bereaved parents whose sorrow has softened and who have found fresh hope and strength for living.

The Compassionate Friends has prepared an informative guide to help in understanding grief. It is given below, in the hope that other parents will benefit from the insight it provides.

UNDERSTANDING GRIEF

Grief, with its many ups and downs, lasts far longer than society in general recognizes. Be patient with yourself.

Each person's grief is individual. You and your spouse will experience it and cope with it differently.

Crying is an acceptable and healthy expression of grief and releases built-up tension for mothers, fathers, brothers and sisters. Cry freely as you feel the need.

Physical reactions to the death of a child may include loss of appetite or overeating, sleeplessness, and sexual difficulties. Parents may find that they have very little energy and cannot concentrate. A balanced diet, rest, and moderate exercise are especially important for the whole family at this time.

Avoid the use of drugs and alcohol. Medication should be taken sparingly and only under the supervision of your physician. Many substances are addictive and can lead to a chemical dependence. In addition they may stop or delay the necessary grieving process.

Friends and relatives may be uncomfortable around you. They want to ease your pain but do not know how. Take the initiative and help them learn how to be supportive to you. Talk about your child so they know this is appropriate.

Whenever possible, put off major decisions (changing residence, changing job, etc.) for at least a year.

Avoid making hasty decisions about your child's belongings. Do not allow others to take over or to rush you. You can do it little by little whenever you feel ready.

Parents may feel they have nothing to live for and may think about a release from this intense pain. Be assured that many parents feel this way but that a sense of purpose and meaning does return. The pain does lessen.

Guilt, real or imagined, is a normal part of grief. It surfaces in thoughts and feelings of "if only." In order to resolve this guilt, learn to express and share these feelings, and learn to forgive yourself.

Anger is another common reaction to loss. Anger, like guilt, needs expression and sharing in a healthy and acceptable manner.

Children are often the forgotten grievers within a family. They are experiencing many of the same emotions you are, so share thoughts and tears with them. Though it is a painful time, be sure they feel loved and included.

Holidays and the anniversaries of your child's birth and death can be stressful times. Consider the feelings of the entire family in planning how to spend the day. Allow time and space for your own emotional needs.

A child's death often causes a parent to challenge and examine his faith or philosophy of life. Don't be disturbed if you are questioning old beliefs. Talk about it. For many, faith offers help to accept the unacceptable.

It helps to become involved with a group of parents having similar experiences; sharing eases loneliness and promotes the expression of your grief in an atmosphere of acceptance and understanding.

BEREAVED PARENTS AND THEIR FAMILIES CAN FIND HEALING AND HOPE FOR THE FUTURE AS THEY REORGANIZE THEIR LIVES IN A POSITIVE WAY.

To provide help to the medical profession, The Compassionate Friends has prepared suggestions for doctors and nurses:

THE COMPASSIONATE FRIENDS SUGGESTIONS FOR DOCTORS AND NURSES

—Prepare parents and siblings for what they will see *before they see it.* Explain beforehand the machines, tubes, needles, etc. Clean and bandage all you can before they come in.

—If parents really want to watch, let them see what you are doing with their child. Let them lead in that decision. (They don't see the same things you see.)

—Anticipate their questions as much as possible. Avoid complicated terminology, but don't "talk down" to families either.

—ALWAYS TELL THE TRUTH! Tell them everything you *know* about their child's condition. Be honest about what you don't know. Tell them the numbers; i.e., blood pressure, temperature, pulse, etc.

—Let parents "parent"—they need to participate in the care of their sick child as much as possible. Later they need to be able to say, "I helped!"

—Give parents permission to talk about their feelings, to be extremely tired, to CRY. Cry with them if you are truly sad. Don't hide your feelings to protect them. You are in a position of authority and your permission (and modeling) gives their feelings validity.

—Parents may not be accepting of bad news, and may cope by denial. Do be patient with parents as denial is a form of emotional protection and will disappear when an individual is ready. Everyone is on a different timetable. Recognize that sometimes there is a need to repeat the same explanation or information several different times; parents in stress may only absorb a little of what you thought had been explained to them.

—Reassure families that everything possible is being done. They won't automatically know or assume that. *Keep* on reassuring them that no measure will be left untried in the attempt to save their child's life.

—Take pictures of newborns who die and put them in the file in case parents want them in future weeks or months. (Many will.)

—Make EVERY EFFORT to arrange for parents to be with the child at the moment of death *if they want to be there.* Please don't "protect" parents from this opportunity. It will be extremely important in their later healing.

—Refer to the child by name—especially after death.

—Remember the two things which concern parents most: "Was my child in pain?" and, "Was my child afraid?" Be prepared to reassure as honestly as possible about these questions.

—Treat parents equally in giving information and breaking news. Fathers need as much support as mothers.

—Families judge you by your caring levels, as well as your medical skills. Convince them their child is special to you, that this is not "just a job."

—Allow parents as much time as they need to be with their child (alone if they want) after death. This is vital in their healing process.

—At the time of informing parents that their child has died, tell them what steps to take next. They are in shock (and disbelief) and will be confused and need direction and guidance. There is no such thing as an "expected death" when it happens!

—Express your personal frustrations: "We try so hard, but sometimes nothing works." "He was such a wonderful child. It hurts us, too, that we couldn't save him."

—Touching is our most basic form of comfort and communication—put your hand on their arm, or your arm around their shoulder.

—If possible, go to the visitation or funeral. It means more than you can imagine. Families will really appreciate your *showing* your caring!

—Most of the parents we've talked with have appreciated being asked about organ transplants. Parents who weren't asked felt left out or even insulted. However, parents need reassurance that their child's body will be treated with respect and dignity.

—Don't expect the parents of a dying child to be logical or objective. Runaway emotions have left logic at the starting gate, and it will take quite a while to catch up!

—Don't "hit and run." If you must break sad news, don't rush away immediately. If you can't handle the situation sensitively, send or take along someone who can.

—Don't assume all anger is "displaced." Some of it is, but some is justified and needs to be ventilated and examined.

—Don't try to give parents rationalizations about their child's death, such as: "Your child would have been a burden to you as he was," or "She just would have suffered if she had lived." (This is the "You're really lucky he died" routine.)

—Don't say "You ought to be feeling better by now," or anything else which implies a judgment about their feelings.

—Don't point out that they can always have another child, or suggest that they should be grateful for their other children. Children are not interchangeable—they cannot replace each other.

—Don't suggest "busy work" as grief therapy. Bereaved people know they need to have something to do, but they are extraordinarily tired for a long time, and whatever they do needs to have meaning and importance.

—Don't be in a hurry to offer medication. There is a big difference between profound sadness and true depression. *Sad* people are often medicated for depression unnecessarily!

REMEMBER: AS YOU TREAT THE PATIENT *IN* THE BED, YOU MUST BE CAREFUL NOT TO CREATE PATIENTS *AROUND* THE BED!

GOLD STAR MOTHERS

On June 4, 1928, twenty-five mothers who lived in Washington, D.C., made plans for a national organization to be known as American Gold Star Mothers, Inc., a nondenominational, nonprofit, and nonpolitical organization. By 1929 it had a membership of sixty-five, including mothers throughout the United States. Later many small groups of Gold Star Mothers functioning under local and state charters became affiliated with the larger national group, with representation in nearly every state. This group was composed of women who had lost a son or daughter in World War I.

At the 1941 national convention the membership was opened to mothers who had lost a son or daughter in World War II and was again opened after the Korean conflict. The objects of this organization are:

> to keep alive and develop the spirit that promoted world service, to maintain the ties of fellowship born of that service and to assist and further all patriotic works, to inculcate a sense of individual obligation to the Community, State, and Nation, to assist veterans and their dependents whenever possible and to aid, in any way in our power, men and women who were wounded or incapacitated, to perpetuate the memory of those whose lives were sacrificed, to extend needful assistance to all Gold Star Mothers and to maintain true allegiance to the United States of America. This is an organization of mothers whose sons or daughters served and died that this world might be a better place in which to live.

The last Sunday in September is designated "Gold Star Mothers' Day," and it is the duty of the president of the United States to request its observance, as a a public expression of the love, sorrow, and reverence of the people of the United States for the American Gold Star Mothers.

There are now more than 600 chapters of American Gold Star Mothers in the United States. Should further information be desired, write to:

American Gold Star Mothers, Inc.
National Headquarters
2128 Leroy Place, NW
Washington, D.C. 20008

THE NATIONAL TAY-SACHS &
ALLIED DISEASES ASSOCIATION

The Tay-Sachs baby appears normal at birth and seems to develop normally until it is about six months old. Initial signs vary and become evident at differing ages in children affected by the disease. A first indication can be a loss of peripheral vision, a slowdown of development, or exhibition of an abnormal startle response. By the time they are one year of age most children suffer recurring convulsions with diminishing ability of the brain to function. The infant begins to regress and one by one starts to lose skills, such as the ability to sit, to crawl, to turn over, to reach out. Deterioration continues as nerve destruction proceeds. There is a progressive inability to swallow and inadequate pulmonary function. With increased loss of coordination, seizures also occur. Ultimately the child is blind, mentally retarded, paralyzed, and no longer in contact with the outside world. Costs for nursing care of a prolonged nature—provided that couples desire hospitalization and if appropriate facilities are available—can approach $60,000 yearly. Financial assistance is often required because families generally are unable to bear such costs. Death inevitably occurs, usually between the ages of three and five.

Educational literature on Tay-Sachs disease is provided by the NTSAD Association, which also acts as a referral agency for families with stricken children. Parents who have had a Tay-Sachs child provide peer-group support for families. The association stresses prevention of Tay-Sachs disease through public educational programs, screening tests for the carrier state of Tay-Sachs disease, and a program of genetic counseling.

Tay-Sachs disease is transmitted as an autosomal recessive disorder—that is, it is transmitted through the genes much the same as hair color and eye color are passed from parent to child. In order to have a Tay-Sachs baby, both parents must be carriers of the recessive TSD gene. Carrier status does not affect the mother and father physically in any way. A person who is a carrier can transmit a particular genetic trait to an offspring but is not ill with the disease. Recessive genetic diseases like Tay-Sachs often occur more frequently, though not exclusively, in a defined population.

Tay-Sachs most often appears in families with no prior history of the disease. Historically it was not uncommon for a woman in the small towns of Europe to bear from six to eight children. Infant mortality rates were high, and sophisticated medical diagnosis was unavailable. It was not unusual for some of these children not to survive beyond two or three years of age. In retrospect the association believes some of these children may have died of Tay-Sachs disease. Recent medical discoveries offer hope of averting tragedy for young couples, who unsuspectingly carry the gene for Tay-Sachs.

Parent peer groups meet in central locations. The parent network provides strong emotional support as well as helps one another care for the child, understand the manifold problems, and receive input from other parents via the phone or in person. Once parents contact the national office, they are asked if they wish to speak to a parent who has had a similar experience. If so, they are put in touch with one or more parents who have lost a child or are going through it now. Many parents live in isolated areas, feeling very alone in their situation and not having anyone who truly understands. The need to reach out and not to feel so isolated is extremely important. An example of the importance of the phone network is a current one: A family in northern Michigan, a family in West Virginia, and another in northern Florida had no one to talk to—until they were in touch with other parents undergoing the same problems.

Should additional information be desired, contact:

National Tay-Sachs & Allied Diseases Association, Inc.
92 Washington Avenue
Cedarhurst, NY 11516
(516) 569-4300

PARENTS OF MURDERED CHILDREN

To families so cruelly bereaved, Parents of Murdered Children (POMC) provides help to any parent who has endured this tragedy. For those who have endured or are enduring the horror of such a loss, POMC offers help to parents troubled about any aspect of their child's murder. A self-help group, the parents affiliated with POMC believe strongly that "a person who has recovered from a problem can be far more helpful than a professional using only theoretical knowledge. Second, when an individual helps another without charge, they both benefit."

Families of a homicide death have to bear an additional burden to the grief process—that of intrusions into their intense grief. The news media may focus on the victim and the grieving family. Police, lawyers, and others in the criminal justice system may require information, testimony, evidence, etc. Whether a murder suspect is apprehended or not, there is further pain. There are trials, sentences pronounced, hearings, postponements—all taking their toll on the grieving parents. Parents of Murdered Children offers ongoing emotional support for parents by phone or mail, in person, one to one, in group meetings, and through literature. The parents in POMC will telephone or write any parent of a murdered child and, if possible, put that parent in touch with others in the vicinity who have survived the homicide of a child. They also will aid any interested parents of a murdered child in forming a chapter of POMC in the community they live. POMC also offers to communicate with any professional in the field of law enforcement, mental health, community services, social work, law, criminal justice, medicine, education, religion, and mortuary science who is interested in learning more about survivors of homicide and their problems. A list of chapters of POMC appears at the back of this book in the Directory of Helping Organizations. Should you wish additional information, contact:

Parents of Murdered Children, Inc.
1739 Bella Vista
Cincinnati, Ohio 45237
Telephone: (513) 242-8025

SHARE (*S*ources of *H*elp in *A*iring and *R*esolving *E*xperiences)

The anguish of young parents who lose infants soon after birth is devastating. Until recently most hospitals were unprepared to deal with the despair of these couples. Today many new approaches have been initiated to help young grief-stricken parents. The first support group for parents whose infants had died was formed at St. John's Hospital in Springfield, Illinois, under the direction of Sister Jane Marie Lamb. The group is called SHARE, and that is its purpose—for young bereaved parents to be able to share their feelings. Subsequently, chapter after chapter of SHARE, and similar groups such as AMEND, Unite, Hoping, Care, Bereaved Parents, Caretakers, Cure, ILAC, T.L.C., P.A.C.E.S., Wee Care, Pend, AIID, Sharing Heart, Kinder-Mourn, Hopes, Hand, etc. have been springing up throughout the country. A listing of these by state appears in the back of this book in the Directory of Helping Organizations. The following information was provided by St. John's:

SHARE holds that in our society grief at the loss of a newborn or after a miscarriage is not acceptable, especially after a week or two. The thought that the infant was never held, coddled, fed, or perhaps embraced causes great pain to the young couples but is often seen by others as a reason for not feeling a loss. Well-meaning relatives and medical personnel may try to protect the grieving mother and father by not talking about the baby; by making plans without including the mother (funeral arrangements, putting away the baby clothes and crib, etc.); by not letting either parent see or hold the baby; or by avoiding naming the baby, etc.

People intimate that it is abnormal to talk about the baby or to have feelings about the child. Those feelings are then held inside and guarded. Time doesn't always heal them because they are not released, and the more time that lapses the less acceptable it is to express these feelings. No parent should have to go through this experience alone. The basic reason for SHARE is the comfort and mutual reassurance that parents who have had this experience can offer each other. The mother and father experiencing this loss need as much, if not more, pampering, concern, affection and attention as the new parents whose baby has survived. The mother also needs, through her treatment by the people around her, to be assured that this is something that *happened* to her, that she is not in any way to blame, nor is she incompetent as a woman. She needs to be encouraged to take good care of herself physically, even though it may be very difficult to love herself in this situation. The father, too, may tend to blame himself. He needs an opportunity to share his feelings and to receive understanding and support.

Through the local SHARE meetings, members *can share* their experiences, thoughts and feelings. Parents learn that the intensity and longevity of their feelings are normal. They gain a sense of wholeness when they realize their problems are not unique to them alone, but rather problems with which most bereaved parents are struggling. SHARE is not a therapy group, nor are these meetings "therapy" sessions. Yet healing is slowly and gently promoted as parents gain insight and understanding, have an opportunity to ventilate their feelings in an accepting atmosphere, and reach out to the newly bereaved. Individuals may express their religious feelings, attitudes, or experiences in group discussions. However, SHARE is non-denominational. What is important is an acceptance of each individual as he or she is.

The impetus to organize this group came from one determined, bereaved parent. From her recognized need and that of others, the idea grew. In order to begin, a committee was formed in late 1977. It consisted of the grieving parent who had come to St. John's, nurses from labor and delivery, postpartum, high-risk neonatal center, and the gynecological unit; social workers; a neonatalogist; and pastoral care personnel. This committee discussed bonding, grief, needs of parents, and personal responses to loss.

In early 1978, parents began attending meetings. At first, only the women attended, but now either both parents come together, one may come alone or bring another "significant support person." Core members of SHARE set the atmosphere at meetings, which are begun by brief introductions by each parent. Ground rules [below] are then read, after which a core member or resident physician gives a short presentation on grief at the loss of a newborn. Then the parents respond—to what they have and are experiencing, and to each other.

Some parents come to the meetings only once, others come over a long period. And still others continue with the group to give support to the newly bereaved. A few of these parents have written a brochure which will hopefully provide help to parents at the time of a baby's death. And others have become involved in producing a video-tape on grief.

The ground rules for meetings established by St. John's SHARE group are as follows:

1. Each of your experiences is unique and valid. No one is here to criticize or analyze.
2. Feel free to share or not share your feelings and experiences. We will not probe. If you have had a similar experience and care to talk about it, feel free to do so.
3. Note pads are available for you to write down any word or phrase which comes to mind. It is okay to write while others are talking; notes are for yourself and you will not be asked to share them.
4. It is okay to cry—there are tissues available and we ask that you be sensitive to your neighbor's needs. We ask your permission to cry, too.
5. If you feel the need to leave, feel free to go. One of us will follow you out of the room, to be sure that before you leave you are ready to drive.
6. Share your feelings about the meeting with your spouse— we do not want to create a communication gap, but rather increase communication.
7. The group time is not intended as a time for medical advice—if you have medical questions, we will respond to them after the general meeting.
8. Should you wish to share a bad experience you have had with a hospital, nurse or doctor, feel free to relate the experience. We would ask that you not use the name in the discussion.
9. The tape recorder will be on for the speaker's presentation only.
10. After the short presentation, you may respond to what the speaker has said or open with anything you wish to bring up. We encourage you to respond to each other.

To provide information to other hospitals and to enlighten those interested in helping bereaved parents, the following excerpts are from correspondence with Sister Jane Marie Lamb of St. John's Hospital. The information therein may well serve as guidelines:

"Since 1973 I have worked in the hospital Pastoral Care Department in a role similar to the chaplain's. My work has put me in contact with many families of critically ill and dying children in Pediatrics, as well as parents whose babies died through miscarriage, stillbirth, or as a newborn before dismissal from the nursery.

"As parents expressed a need for support beyond the hospitalization period, I began to work toward a self-help support group. SHARE became a reality in 1978 and through continuing contact with these parents in the group I have gained new sensitivities and insights into the parents' pain and subsequent needs. I also attend The Compassionate Friends meetings as a support person and follow up with many I have known during hospitalization of their child.

"During a child's hospitalization I spend a great deal of time with the parents. If the child is terminally ill I try to help the parents to cope. I do not take away hope, but help them deal with reality. I feel that honesty and openness is important. I keep in touch with their wishes and coping abilities.

"After a child dies I am there to listen and provide support. That will vary with each circumstance. I allow other family members and friends to be that support person if they are present, as they will be with the family in the days and weeks to come. I try to help the support person know ways they can be of help. We talk about ways that they might continue to be supportive.

"I try to help them be with the dying child, to hold the child, to have pictures and remembrances of the newborn, to provide time alone, to encourage naming the baby (if it is not yet named) and to discuss the funeral and how it can be meaningful. Often I will discuss the grief process and what they may experience, how others may respond or fail to respond to them and what resources are available—professional staff members, other bereaved parents on a one-to-one basis, support groups such as the two mentioned above, our newsletter and their physicians. I write to many of them, talk with them over the phone, and visit them individually when possible.

"I do attend SHARE meetings as a facilitator. In that role I do not take an active part, once the meetings are under way. I open the meetings and introduce the speaker, or give the presentation, then encourage the parents to relate to each other. Often I will talk with individual parents after the meeting and offer support as they work through a difficult situation they discussed at the session.

"How do I handle the immediate effect on the parents? I try to be with them and respond to them individually, as each parent will differ in expression of grief. I am there. In some instances I may say and do very little other than pick up on needs and requests. I try to provide opportunities to begin the grief process and facilitate their seeing and holding the child.

"Sometimes we will talk about the child, the memories they have and the things that will *now* be important. I talk to them about not trying to forget the child—he will always be important in their lives. I talk about how difficult it is to give up their precious child. This will vary as some are very quiet while others are very verbal.

"Privacy for the grieving parents is very important. It is difficult to be near others who have a child recovering. We provide privacy and even try to be sensitive as to whether the parents want other relatives or would prefer to be alone during this period. In our High Risk Nursery area we have a family room with beds, so that a newly delivered mother can have a place to rest, and yet be close to her critically ill baby. We bring the dead baby to this room afterward, so that the parents have privacy.

"Some parents find support within their own family and circle of friends. Most other couples will find the support they need by contact with the self-help group or contact with another couple with whom they identify. There is an occasional situation in the follow-up period where we recommend that the couple see a professional person. They are given our calling card with the names of three people within the hospital staff they can call.

"I encourage them to make note of the name of any nurse they feel would be helpful to them. They are free to call any of us.

"We send the parents a letter the middle of the month following the loss. This time lapse allows them opportunity to have worked through some of the shock and numbness that they may have experienced at the beginning of the loss. Dr. Glen Davidson, a grief specialist from Southern Illinois University School of Medicine, indicates they are most responsive to receiving help when they are in the stage of searching and yearning. I have seen parents come as soon as four days after the death of their child, while other wait for a couple of years. The average person waits a month or two before they come to the realization that support of others could help them.

"Parents who are having greater difficulties are at times referred to a psychologist or counselor. If I feel that additional help would be helpful I related to them on a one to one basis. In our situation many of the parents are familiar with Dr. Davidson through his occasional participation in the group session, as well as through his films. Many however will choose not to seek the additional help. Others want a longer period before coming to realize that seeking professional help would facilitate the grief process more effectively.

"Since the group is getting older, there are many parents who help with the follow up. Ideally we would like to follow each parent who has had a loss. The social workers contact by phone all who have lost a child in the High Risk Center. The neonatologist sees them after six weeks to answer questions, to evaluate what has happened in their adjustment and processing of grief, and take this opportunity to discuss the autopsy report if any autopsy has been performed.

"Parents from the group call each other between meetings. Friends and relatives often call me if they are concerned.

There are several ways we handle the follow-up, but we are not staffed to adequately follow each family.

"I find that by reaching out to other parents these parents heal more quickly. The bond between the parents and others in a similar situation becomes strong and develops more easily than the average relationship. Helping other parents is a gift to their baby.

"Our group has taken meals to parents who have had to be bedfast during part of the pregnancy or have offered to care for the children. They have given blankets to be used for babies who die, they have made ornaments for Christmas so that the bereaved parent will have a remembrance of their dead babies.

"Many of our parents write parents in other states. I have a long list of parents who are willing to help others. Several are willing to talk to groups, medical students, or anyone willing to know more about grief. They have now taken over the newsletter, and have contributed 90 percent of the content for some time. I really can't enumerate all that the parents have done and the great need they feel to be involved. Early in the loss they were overwhelmed by their own pain, but as time goes on they want to reach out to others. Some parents are ready to reach out earlier than others, so I feel it is important to leave that to them."

Should any additional information concerning SHARE be needed write to:

SHARE
St. John's Hospital
800 East Carpenter
Springfield, Illinois 62769
Telephone: (217) 544-6464

SUDDEN INFANT DEATH SYNDROME GROUPS

There are three organizations concerned with the problem of Sudden Infant Death Syndrome: the National Sudden Infant

Death Syndrome Foundation, the Council of Guilds for Infant Survival, and the Sudden Infant Death Syndrome Information and Counseling Program. Both the NSIDS Foundation and the Council of Guilds for Infant Survival are organizations which were started in the 1960s by parents of SIDS victims. There is a network of local chapters throughout the country, made up of volunteer SIDS parents and concerned community members. The goals of both parent groups are:

1. To support medical research into the cause and prevention of Sudden Infant Death Syndrome.
2. To help parents of SIDS victims understand what is known about this mysterious disease so that they will not feel unwarranted guilt over the death of their child.
3. To train health professionals to assist SIDS families in their time of loss.
4. To educate the public and professional community so that misunderstanding of SIDS may be eradicated.

Helping the SIDS Family

While medical research continues, SIDS also continues to claim the lives of thousands of babies each year. The aftermath of a SIDS death is overwhelming grief and guilt: grief because a loved one is gone; guilt because parents often blame themselves for the death of the infant. The parents' groups support the training and activities of health professionals who help SIDS families understand that SIDS is neither preventable nor predictable—and that parents are not to blame for the death of their child. Volunteer SIDS parents provide families with the sympathetic understanding they desperately need in a time of great personal loss. Chapter members stand by ready to telephone, visit, or counsel grief-stricken parents at any time, even in the hospital emergency room.

Public Education

Because so little is known about SIDS, it is essential that what is known be distributed to SIDS parents, health professionals, emergency medical personnel, and the public at large. The parents' groups sponsor educational programs and seminars to eradicate misunderstanding about SIDS and to sensitize health professionals and the general community to the needs of SIDS families.

Government Funding

The Sudden Infant Death Syndrome Information and Counseling Program was established in 1974 by the SIDS Act, P.L. 93–270. It is administered by the Office of Maternal and Child Health in the Bureau of Community Health Services. The purpose of the SIDS Information and Counseling Program is to provide funds for projects which include the collection, analysis, and furnishing of information relating to the syndrome and for the counseling of bereaved families. The objectives of the program provide for autopsies in all sudden, unexpected deaths of children up to one year of age, certification of SIDS on the death certificate, and prompt notification of the parent about the cause of death, preferably within twenty-four to forty-eight hours.

A primary purpose of the program is to provide counseling services to families that have lost an infant to SIDS. Also called crib death, this tragedy occurs when the baby, appearing to be perfectly healthy in most cases, is put to bed and later is found dead from no visible causes. Many theories are postulated, but none offers consolation to anguished parents who feel responsible: "I didn't look in on the baby enough ... The covers must have smothered her ... I didn't go in when he was crying." In some way, the parents believe they must have been careless, or how could this have happened? Doctors explain that these self-accusations are not unusual in a bereaved parent whose child has died in a crib death. Discussion with other SIDS parents, or counseling, can relieve parents of many of their guilt feelings. It has also been found that an autopsy report can help allay the fears parents have that they were careless or that the baby suffocated or choked as a result of inattention. While programs vary according to location, some of the activities may include:

1. Counseling
   a. Crisis intervention of SIDS families.
   b. Telephone counseling.
   c. Referral services.
2. Parent Support
   a. Parents are invited to attend parents' meetings.
   b. Parents may call other parents who have experienced the loss of a child to SIDS.
3. Home Visits
   Through the department of health, public health nurses visit each family in their home after the infant's death to discuss SIDS and to offer whatever other help may be needed.
4. Education
   Community education programs are provided to agencies and persons that have direct and considerable influence on the nature and duration of the parents' grief, such as police departments, fire departments, ambulance corps, and hospital emergency rooms.
5. Information
   Literature about SIDS is available to parents, agencies, and interested persons.

For more information, contact:

The National Clearinghouse for SIDS
Suite 600
1555 Wilson Boulevard
Rosslyn, Virginia 22209
Telephone: (703) 522-0870

or

The National SIDS Foundation
2 Metro Plaza
Suite 205
8240 Professional Place
Landover, Maryland 20785
Telephone: (301) 459-3388

or

National Headquarters
Council of Guilds for Infant Survival
P.O. Box 3841
Davenport, Iowa 52808

11 · Directory of Helping Organizations

The following directory of helping groups is to provide information for bereaved families. The chapters and centers listed are comprised often of names of parents who currently head them. Inasmuch as these can change every few years, if there is any question, contact the national headquarters or national clearinghouse where listed.

PEER GROUPS

THE COMPASSIONATE FRIENDS, INC.

The Compassionate Friends is a self-help organization for bereaved parents. A bereaved parent contacting the main office indicated below will be responded to individually and, whenever possible, will also be referred to the name, address, and phone of the closest local chapter leader. Because of the changes that take place in telephone numbers and addresses, and to insure a bereaved parent of the latest and most accurate referral information in his/her area, *all inquiries* are to be directed to:

The Compassionate Friends, Inc.
National Headquarters
P.O. Box 1347
Oak Brook, Illinois 60521

Should you wish any additional information, a volunteer is available weekdays from 10:00 A.M. to 3:00 P.M. CST at (312) 323-5010 and would be happy to talk to you.

The Compassionate Friends has almost 300 chapters throughout the United States, as well as abroad. The following list indicates some of the cities, with more being added daily as a result of the rapid expansion of this fine organization, the goal of which is to lighten the burden of grief for bereaved parents, offering friendship and understanding.

Chapters of Compassionate Friends

ALABAMA
Birmingham
Huntsville
Mobile
Montgomery
Opelika
Tuscaloosa

ARKANSAS
El Dorado
Fort Smith

ARIZONA
Globe-Miami
Phoenix

CALIFORNIA
Alameda County/San Francisco
Fresno
Glendale
Los Angeles/Lawndale
Los Angeles/San Fernando Valley
Los Banos
Palm Desert
Palo Alto/San Jose
Pomona Valley/San Gabriel
Sacramento
San Diego
San Francisco
San Rafael
Santa Clarita Valley
Van Nuys
Ventura
Walnut Creek

COLORADO
Colorado Springs
Denver
Fort Collins
Grand Junction
Greeley
Montrose
Nunn

CONNECTICUT
Bridgeport
Groton
Hartford
New Haven
Rockville
Stamford

FLORIDA
Clearwater
Fort Walton Beach
Lakeland
Miami
Miami/Fort Lauderdale
New Port Richey
Orange Park
Orlando
Sarasota
Tallahassee
Tampa
Titusville
West Palm Beach

GEORGIA
Albany
Atlanta
Bremen
Canton
North Atlanta
Warner Robins

HAWAII
Honolulu
Kahului

IDAHO
Boise
Burley

ILLINOIS
Alton/Moro
Arlington Heights
Aurora

Champaign/Urbana
Chicago
Decatur
Fenton
Hinsdale
Joliet
Mattoon
Mendota
Park Forest
Rockford
Springfield
Waukegan
Wilmette

INDIANA
Anderson
Carmel/Indianapolis
Elkhart
Evansville
Fort Wayne
Greenwood
Kendallville
La Porte
Logansport
Moores Hill
South Bend
Valparaiso
Vincennes
Wabash

IOWA
Albia
Davenport
Des Moines
Indianola
Marshalltown
Sioux City
Waterloo/Cedar Falls

KANSAS
Garden City
Kansas City
Topeka
Wichita

KENTUCKY
Bowling Green
Henderson
Lexington
Louisville
Owensboro
Paducah

LOUISIANA
Shreveport

MARYLAND
Baltimore
Salisbury/Delmarva
St. Leonard
Walkersville
Wheaton

MASSACHUSETTS
Hingham
Needham/Boston
North Reading/Boston
Springfield
Worcester

MICHIGAN
Alpena
Ann Arbor
Benton Harbor
Big Rapids
Detroit
Grand Rapids
Jackson
Lansing
Saginaw
Traverse City

MINNESOTA
Crookston
Detroit Lakes
Fairmont
Minneapolis
New Ulm
St. Cloud
Willmar

MISSISSIPPI
Gulfport
Jackson

MISSOURI
Columbia
Independence
Jefferson City
Joplin
Kansas City
Mexico
St. Joseph
St. Louis
Springfield

MONTANA
Billings
Eureka
Hamilton
Kalispell

NEBRASKA
Chadron
Omaha
Scottsbluff

NEVADA
Carson City
Las Vegas

NEW HAMPSHIRE
Durham

NEW JERSEY
Audubon
Brookside
Flemington
Holmdel
Princeton
South Plainfield
Spotswood
Teaneck
Toms River
Verona

NEW MEXICO
Albuquerque
Gallup

NEW YORK
Buffalo
Clayton
Delmar/Albany
Geneseo/Naples
Kingston
Long Island/New York
New York City
Niagara Falls
Orchard Park
Purdy's Station
Rochester
Suffolk County
Wellsville
West Adirondack-Star Lake

NORTH CAROLINA
Concord
Hickory
Raleigh

NORTH DAKOTA
Bismarck
Grand Forks

OHIO
Akron
Carrollton
Chagrin Falls/Cleveland
Cincinnati
Columbus
Dayton
Huber Heights/Dayton
Mount Vernon
Niles
Parma/Cleveland
Westlake/Cleveland
South Suburban Dayton
St. Henry
Van Wert

OKLAHOMA
Bartlesville
Enid
Norman
Oklahoma City
Stillwater
Tulsa

OREGON
Albany
Eugene
Portland
Roseburg
Salem

PENNSYLVANIA
Ambler
Bala Cynwyd/Philadelphia
Beaver
Carlisle
Conneautville
Ebensburg
Ephrata
Greensburg
Harrisburg
Holicong
Johnstown
Myerstown
Pittsburgh
Pottsville/Schuylkill
Ridgeway
Thompsontown
Warrington
Wilkes-Barre
York

SOUTH CAROLINA
Beaufort
Charleston
Columbia
Greenville

TENNESSEE
Clarksville
Memphis

TEXAS
Abilene
Amarillo
Austin
Beaumont
Borger
Corpus Christi
Dallas
El Paso
Fort Worth
Houston North
Houston Southeast
Houston West
Houston Northwest
Nacogdoches
San Angelo
San Antonio
Victoria

UTAH
Salt Lake City

VERMONT
Brattleboro
Newport
White River Junction
Lyndon Center

VIRGINIA
Burke
Falls Church
Quantico
Richmond
Tazewell

WASHINGTON
Bellingham
Bothell/Seattle
Bremerton
Pullman
Spokane
Tacoma

WEST VIRGINIA
Huntington

WISCONSIN

Appleton
Fond du Lac
Green Bay

Manitowoc
Ripon
Shawano
Waukesha
Whitefish Bay/Milwaukee

PARENTS OF MURDERED CHILDREN

National Headquarters

Parents of Murdered Children
1739 Bella Vista
Cincinnati, OH 45237
Telephone: (513) 242-8025

Current Chapters

ALABAMA
Clyde and Hilda Wolverton
1157 McKenly
Auburn, AL 36830

ALASKA
James and Judy Connolly
Box 10-201
Anchorage, AK 99511

ARIZONA
Stan and Emerine Hopkins
2620 S. Fairfield Street
Tempe, AZ 85282

CALIFORNIA
Contra Costa Chapter
Nancy Bowman
118 Warwick Drive, #32
Benicia, CA 94510

Don and Pat Brown
2513 Recinto Avenue
Rowland Heights, CA 91748
(Los Angeles Area)

Eva Sands
10458 Ambassador Drive
Rancho Cordova, CA 95670
(Sacramento area)

Ed and Janice Batten
3215 Chauncey Drive
San Diego, CA 92123

Peninsula/South Bay Chapter
Jean Lewis
3250 Hedda Court
San Jose, CA 95127

COLORADO
Pat Robinson
228 La Paz Place
Longmont, CO 80501

ILLINOIS
Margaret and Bob Coombs
O.S. 655 Madison Street
Winfield, IL 60190

KENTUCKY
Juanita Lafferre
6905 Hallwood Court
Louisville, KY 40291

MICHIGAN
Judy Thomasen
24801 Cherry
Dearborn, MI 48124

MINNESOTA
Tinka Bloedow
11657 Palmer Road
Bloomington, MN 55437
(Minneapolis/St. Paul area)

NEW YORK
Sidney and Barbara Davis
6 Ridge Rock Lane
East Norwich, NY 11732

OHIO
Robert and Charlotte Hullinger
1739 Bella Vista
Cincinnati, OH 45237

OREGON
Bob and Joan Synarski
4059 N. Overlook Terrace
Portland, OR 97227

PENNSYLVANIA
Frank and Deborah Spungen
101 Naudain Street
Philadelphia, PA 19147

TEXAS
Sara Marsh
2401 Lazy Hollow, Apartment 147A
Houston, TX 77063

James and Louise Burrus
208 Duke
Garland, TX 75043
(Dallas area)

WISCONSIN
Robert and Marge Esser
141 Stuart Road
Racine, WI 53406

CANADA
Donna Bourne
854 Hendecourt Road
North Vancouver, B.C.
V7K-2Y2, Canada

SHARE

Sister Jane Marie Lamb, R.N.
St. John's Hospital
800 E. Carpenter
Springfield, Illinois 62702
Telephone: (217) 544-6464

The following are listings of SHARE and similar support groups. The listings (including AMEND, Unite, Hoping, Care, Hopes, Bereaved Parents, Wee Care, AIID, Pend, Sharing Heart, Kinder-Mourn, Cure, Hand, Caretakers, T.L.C., and others) were provided by St. John's SHARE, with the indication that each of the groups have their own identity: "We have made lists of all the groups we know of in the country. Many have no connection with us, but we wanted to refer people to a group that could help them in their vicinity." SHARE also advises that from time to time the personal contacts at the various groups are subject to change.

In addition, when new chapters form, those in charge are asked to advise the National Self Help Clearinghouse at the address shown below. The Clearinghouse acts as an updated reference center and there is no charge for listing groups.

National Self Help Clearinghouse or
33 West 42 Street
New York, New York 10036
Telephone: (212) 852-4290

National Self Help Resource Center
2000 South Street N.W.
Washington, D.C. 20009
Telephone: (202) 338-5704

(The listings within each state are arranged alphabetically by city.)

SHARE and Similar Support Groups

CALIFORNIA

AMEND (Aiding Mothers'
Experiencing Newborn Death)
Mrs. Robyn Altman
4032 Towhee Drive
Calabasa, CA 91302

SHARE
Diane Bremseth
436 Loverne
Clovis, CA 93612
(209) 299-0008

AMEND
Janid Rangel
247 Granada Avenue
Long Beach, CA 90803

SHARING PARENTS (A SHARE
Group)
Christina Hom
24 Southlite Circle
Sacramento, CA 95831
(916) 392-7925

HAND (Helping After Neonatal
Death)
c/o Barbara Jones
P.O. Box 62
San Anselmo, CA 94960

HAND
P.O. Box 3805
San Francisco, CA 94119

HOPING (Helping Other Parents
in Normal Grieving)
5335 Carita Street
Long Beach, CA 90808

*PARENT BEREAVEMENT
OUTREACH*
Lee Schmidt, R.N.
535 16th Street
Santa Monica, CA 90402

COLORADO
Mary Krugman
ROSE MEDICAL CENTER
4567 E. Ninth Avenue
Denver, CO 80220

*THE GRIEF EDUCATION
INSTITUTE*
P.O. Box 623
Englewood, CO 80001
(303) 777-9234

FLORIDA
HOPES (Helping Other Parents
Experience Sorrow)
Sandi Boston
P.O. Box 1143
Lutz, FL 33549
(813) 933-4720

AMEND
Karen Frazier
5104 127th Ave.
Tampa, FL 33617
(813) 988-7996

IDAHO
COPE (Coping with the Overall
Pregnancy-Parenting Experience)
Laree Larson
Rt. #1
Grace, ID 83241

COPE
Elaine White
Weston, ID 83286
(208) 747-3409

ILLINOIS
SHARE
Sister Mary Ellen Rombach, R.N.
St. Elizabeth Hospital
Pastoral Care Department
211 S. 3rd Street
Belleville, IL 62221

EASE (Empty Arms Support
Effort)
Mary Beth Donnelly
607 E. Olive
Bloomington, IL 61701
(309) 828-8773

SHARE
Debbie Rubach
St. Anthony's Hospital
503 Maple Street
Effingham, IL 62401

SHARE
Sandra Fish
1327 N. Prairie
Galesburg, IL 61401

BARR-HARRIS GRIEF GROUPS
180 N. Michigan Avenue
Chicago, IL 60601
(312) 726-6300

SHARE
Sister Gerard
St. Francis Hospital
1215 E. Union Avenue
Litchfield, IL 62056

SHARE
Gregory and JoAnne Matzke
10301 Medill Road
Melrose Park, IL 60164

CARETAKERS
Rev. Robert L. Hansen
West Suburban Hospital
518 N. Austin Boulevard
Oak Park, IL 60302

SHARE
Shelley Fundell, RSW
Pekin Memorial Hospital
Court and Fourteenth Streets
Pekin, IL 61554
(309) 347-1151

SHARE
Ingrid Peake, R.N.
Blessing Hospital
1005 Broadway
Quincy, IL 62301

SHARE
Our Saviors Lutheran Church
3300 Rural
Rockford, IL 61107

SHARE
Lynda Wilgus
Rockford Memorial Hospital
Social Services
2400 N. Rockton
Rockford, IL 62205

INDIANA
PROJECT COMFORT
Marcia and Greg Schroeder
310 E. 2nd Street
Bloomington, IN 47401
(812) 334-3113

BEREAVED PARENTS GROUPS
Parents and Friends of Children,
Inc.
101 S. Capitol Avenue
Corydon, IN 47112
(812) 738-3277

PROJECT COMFORT
c/o Gerald C. Machgan, Chaplain
Parkview Hospital
2200 Randalia Drive
Fort Wayne, IN 46805
(219) 484-6636

SHARE
Julie Sims
659 N. 7th Street
Lafayette, IN 47901
(317) 742-6574

BEREAVED PARENTS GROUP
Mrs. William Bear
2329 Hargan Drive
Madison, IN 47250

IOWA
SHARE
Debbie Walz
Burlington Medical Center
602 N. Third
Burlington, IA 62601
(319) 753-3011

PARENTS WITH EMPTY ARMS
Jo Marion
1026 A. Avenue NE
St. Lukes Hospital
Cedar Rapids, IA 52402

*PARENTS SHARE AND
SUPPORT*
Mary Olson, RN
112 Jefferson Street
West Union, IA 52175
(319) 422-3811

KENTUCKY
SHARE
Dorothy Van Sant
St. Anthony Hospital
Louisville, KY 40204

MASSACHUSETTS
COPE
37 Claredon Street
Boston, MA 02116
(617) 357-5588

*SUPPORT GROUP FOR
BEREAVED PARENTS*
c/o Pat Berman and Laura Simons
Department of Social Services
Bringham and Women's Hospital
221 Longwood Avenue
Boston, MA 02115

HOPE
c/o Susan Harrington
South Shore Hospital
55 Fogg Road
South Weymouth, MA 02190
(617) 337-7011, Ext. 332

GRIEF SUPPORT GROUP
c/o Linda Brink
P.O. Box 193, West Side Station
Worcester, MA 01602

MICHIGAN
PEND (Parents Experiencing
Neonatal Death)
c/o Neonatal I.C.U.
Marcia Eager
Butterworth Hospital
Grand Rapids, MI 49503

HOPING (Helping Other Parents
In Necessary Grief)
Jeanie Cain
917 Kenwood
Lansing, MI 49503

HOPING
Dess Johnson
E. W. Sparrow Hospital
Department of Social Work
1215 Michigan
Lansing, MI 48910
(517) 483-2385
(517) 483-2344

CARE (Caring and Restoring Each
Other)
George and Kay Brown
13980 East Ridgeville
Ottawa Lake, MI 49267

BEREAVED PARENTS GROUP
c/o Sister Mary Ruth
Providence Hospital
Southfield, MI 48075

MINNESOTA
*PARENTS' GRIEF SUPPORT
GROUP*
c/o Kathy Peterson
St. Mary's Hospital
Duluth, MN 55804
(218) 727-4551, Ext. 384

*PARENTS' GRIEF SUPPORT
GROUP*
4340 London Road
Duluth, MN 55804

MISSOURI
AMEND
Dianne Donahue
16043 Clarkson Woods Drive
Chesterfield, MO 63017
(314) 532-3888

AMEND
Linda McGrath
2164 Golden Rain Drive
Chesterfield, MO 63017
(314) 532-0140

AMEND
Mrs. Peggy Springer
P.O. Box 174
Columbia, MO 65201

HOPE (Helping Other Parents
Endure)
Laura Evans
22 Brixworth
Florissant, MO 63003
(314) 355-1491

HOPE
P.O. Box 153
Florissant, MO 65807

MOTHERS IN CRISIS
Terry Weston
Freeman Hospital
Joplin, MO 62801
(417) 623-2801

AMEND
Mrs. Terry Weston
1310 Fairmont
Neosho, MO 64850

COMPASSIONATE FRIENDS
Sherry Wood
St. John's Hospital
1235 E. Cherokee
Springfield, MO 65802

COMPASSIONATE FRIENDS
Pat Haas
921 Cherry
Springfield, MO 65807

AMEND
Maureen Connelly
4324 Berrywick Terrace
St. Louis, MO 63128

SIDS (Sudden Infant Death
Syndrome)
Helen Fuller
University Club Bldg.
607 N. Grand Boulevard
St. Louis, MO 63101

NEBRASKA
WEE CARE
Rose Estes
1709 W. 38th
Kearney, NE 68847

NEW JERSEY
HELP
Eileen Thompson
Ventnor, NJ 08406
(609) 822-6265

NEW YORK
BEREAVEMENT CLINIC
Nancy O'Donohue
King's County Hospital
451 Clarkson Avenue
Brooklyn, NY 11203
(201) 257-2464

BEREAVEMENT CLINIC
c/o Joanne Middleton
Downstate Medical Center
150 Clarkson Avenue
Brooklyn, NY 11203

GRIEF GROUPS
Dr. Roberta Temes
262 Coleridge Street
Brooklyn, NY 11235
(212) 646-5537

ST. MARY'S BEREAVEMENT MINISTRY
Mrs. Carol Carney
East Islip, NY 11730
(516) 277-4759

SHARE
Lois Sugarman
6726 Gleason Place
Fayetteville, NY 13066
(Syracuse Group)
(315) 446-1262

ST. JOSEPH'S BEREAVEMENT MINISTRY
Sheila Hoffman, Director
130 5th Street
Garden City, NY 11530
(516) 747-7210 (9:00–4:00 P.M.)
(516) 742-1284 (Home)

SHARE
Janet Grutman
4 Hampton Court
Lake Success, NY 11020
(516) 487-5975

ST. PHILLIP'S BEREAVEMENT MINISTRY
Cindy Pinto
Northport, NY 11768
(516) 261-0495

MISCARRIAGE AND STILL-BIRTH SUPPORT GROUP
Dorothy Hai
209 York Street
Olean, NY 14760
(716) 375-2111
(716) 372-7021

T.L.C. (Together in the Loss of a Child)
Laurie Britt, President
29 S. White Street
Poughkeepsie, NY 12601
(914) 473-7995

Melinda Mara, Secretary
1 Morehouse Road
Poughkeepsie, NY 12603
(914) 473-1681

SHARE
Mary C. Wasacz
172 Madison Road
Scarsdale, NY 10583

NORTH CAROLINA
PARENT CARE, INC.
P.O. Box 125
Cary, NC 27511

KINDER-MOURN
6900 Percade Lane
Charlotte, NC 28215

KINDER-MOURN
605 E. Boulevard
Charlotte, NC 28203
(704) 376-2580

OHIO
BEREAVED PARENTS GROUP
Denny and Janie Churchill
3136 Ellet Avenue
Akron, OH 44312
(216) 628-8335

SHARE
Marilyn Miller Graef
1272 Indian Hill Drive
Bolivar, OH 44612
(216) 874-3100

Father Ken Czillinger
ST. MATTHIAS CHURCH
1044 W. Kemper Road
Cincinnati, OH 45240

*RAINBOW BABIES AND
CHILDREN'S HOSPITAL*
2101 Adelbert Road
Cleveland, OH 44106

*PARENTS SUPPORT GROUP
CHILDBIRTH ED.
ASSOCIATION OF AKRON*
c/o Linda Bailey
2183 Larchdale
Guy Falls, OH 44221

CARE (Caring and Restoring Each
Other)
Dr. Irwin Weinfold, M.D.
Northwest Ohio Regional Perinatal
Center
2142 N. Cove Boulevard
Toledo, OH 43606
(419) 473-4224

OKLAHOMA
AMEND
Cindy Wilcox
1344 E. 26th Place
Tulsa, OK 74100

PENNSYLVANIA
SHARE
Mary Anne Eggen
10 Highland Court
Downington, PA 19335

SHARE
Kathy Kuhn
418 Chelsea Drive
Lancaster, PA 17601
(717) 569-6059

BOOTH MATERNITY CENTER
Nancy Jones
6051 Overbrook Avenue
Philadelphia, PA 19131
(215) 878-7800

GRIEVING CLINIC
Temple University Health Science
Center
3401 N. Broad Street
Philadelphia, PA 19140

UNITE
Marion Cohen
2014 Locust Street
Philadelphia, PA 19103
(215) 732-7723

UNITE
Bernadette Foley
Jeane's Hospital
7600 Central Avenue
Philadelphia, PA 19111
(215) 728-2082

Medical Social Work Department
Magee Women's Hospital
Forbes Avenue and Halkea Street
Pittsburgh, PA 15213
(412) 647-4255

SHARE
Donna and Joseph DeLuca
60 Wren Way
Washington, PA 15301
(412) 745-7478

SOUTH CAROLINA
SHARE
Deborah Finley
1110 Hagood Avenue
Columbia, SC 29205
(803) 254-7132

TENNESSEE
PEPD (Parents Experiencing
Perinatal Death)
P.O. Box 38445
Germantown, TN 38138

TEXAS
HAND
Mrs. Karen Riley
14207 Loche Lane
Houston, TX 70077
(713) 493-6792

*BEREAVED PARENTS SUPPORT
GROUP*
Chaplain Raymond Wolfe
Methodist Hospital, P.O. Box 1201
3615 19th Street
Lubbock, TX 79408
(806) 792-1011

SHARE
Constance Clear
534 Avenue B
San Antonio, TX 78209
(512) 822-4135

UTAH
SHARING HEART
Thomas D. Coleman
University of Utah Medical Center
Dept. of Pediatrics, Rm 2B 425
50 N. Medical Drive
Salt Lake City, UT 84132
(801) 581-7052

WASHINGTON
PARENTS OF STILLBORN
Judy Campbell
Group Health Cooperative-
East Side
Redmond, WA 98052
(206) 883-5761

PARENTS OF STILLBORN
Bill and Doreen Volleman
6210 S. 120th Street
Seattle, WA 98178
(206) 772-5338

WISCONSIN
BEREAVED PARENTS GROUP
St. Joseph's Hospital
2661 County Trunk I
Chippewa Falls, WI 54729

SHARE
Mari VandenBerg
St. Vincent's Hospital
P.O. Box 1220
Green Bay, WI 54305
(414) 433-8261

RESOLVE THROUGH SHARING
Carolyn Smiley
Lutheran Hospital
1910 South Avenue
6th Floor Maternity
LaCrosse, WI 54601
(608) 785-0530

SHARE
St. Francis Medical Center
700 West Avenue South
LaCrosse, WI 54601
(608) 785-0940

THE BEREAVED PARENT GROUP
Carol and Don Fowler
1016 Van Vuren Street
Madison, WI 53711
(608) 257-6352

AIID (Aid In Infants Death)
P.O. Box 20852
Milwaukee, WI 53220

SHARE
Mary Koczan
St. Nicholas Hospital
2419 Seaman Avenue
Sheboygan, WI 53081
(414) 459-8300

PARENTS SUPPORTING PARENTS
c/o Rice Clinic
Mary Berg
2501 Main Street
Stevens Point, WI 54481

BEREAVED PARENTS GROUP
Joel and Rae Ann Sigal
409 Lake View Drive
Wausau, WI 54401

SUDDEN INFANT DEATH SYNDROME CHAPTERS IN U.S.A.

Headquarters:
Council of Guilds for Infant
Survival
P.O. Box 3841
Davenport, Iowa 52808

Contacts for Other Chapters:

Dr. Tommy Chase
1206 Ferndale Drive
Auburn, Alabama 36830

Peggy Sisson
1825 Wagner Street
Pasadena, California 91107

Jeane Davies
1172 Lynbrook Way
San Jose, California 95129

Linda Lynch
1635 Laurel Street
South Pasadena, California 91030

Chris Elliott
P.O. Box 35
Yorba Linda, California 92686

So. Illinois G.I.S.
P.O. Box 1116
Centralia, Illinois 62801

Iowa Guild for Infant Survival
P.O. Box 3586
Davenport, Iowa

Northeast Iowa Guild
P.O. Box 1274
Waterloo, Iowa 50704

Millie Thatcher
8074 Phirne Road East
Glen Burnie, Maryland 21061

Sandy Paris
Box 488, Route 14
Pasadena, Maryland 21122

Saul Goldberg
9706 Mendoza Road
Randallstown, Maryland 21133

Kay Rumford
150 W. Park Avenue
Oaklyn, New Jersey 08107

Joan Hornbeck
14830 S. Fernbluff Drive
Oregon City, Oregon 97045

Janie Cram
2716 NE Skidmore
Portland, Oregon 97211

Joseph W. Priddy
2407 Third Avenue
Altoona, Pennsylvania 16602

Donna Shubrooks
1331 Wabank Road
Lancaster, Pennsylvania 17603

Central Penna., G.I.S.
c/o Jackie and John Souders
R.D. #3, 519 Saw Mill Road
Mechanicsburg, Pennsylvania 17055

Philadelphia Chapter, Pa. G.I.S.
1729 Stanwood Street
Philadelphia, Pennsylvania 19152

June Aldren
Jolley Funeral Home
Box 118
Sturgis, South Dakota 57785

Nina Copp
2956 Eric Lane
Farmers Branch, Texas 75234

Scott Hessek
5300 W. Norfolk Road
Portsmouth, Virginia 23703

Catherine Lively
8781 Riverside Drive
Richmond, Virginia 23235

Nils Melherson
420 Forest Hill Crescent
Suffolk, Virginia 23434

Alison Bearse
9913 Vale Road
Vienna, Virginia 22180

Information and Counseling Project Grants

STATE	GRANTEE	CONTACT PERSONS
Alabama	SIDS Information and Counseling Project Alabama Department of Public Health Bureau of Maternal and Child Health/FP State Office Building Montgomery, AL 36130	Beverly Boyd, M.D. Project Director (205) 932-6525 Fern Shinbaum, R.N. Project Coordinator (205) 832-6546

Arkansas	SIDS Information and Counseling Project Arkansas Department of Health Maternal and Child Health Division 4815 W. Markham Little Rock, AR 72201	J. B. Norton, M.D. Project Director (501) 378-0498 Cindy Krone, R.N., C.P.N.P. Project Coordinator (Acting) (501) 661-2747
California	SIDS Information and Counseling Project California Department of Health Services Maternal and Child Health Section 2151 Berkeley Way, Annex 4 Berkeley, CA 94704	Lyn Headley, M.D. Project Director (415) 540-2098 Judith K. Grether, Ph.D. Project Coordinator (415) 540-2108
Colorado	SIDS Information and Counseling Project Colorado Department of Health Child Health Services Division 4210 E. Eleventh Avenue Denver, CO 80220	Barbara Cabela, R.N. Project Director (313) 320-6137, Ext. 338 (Vacant) Project Coordinator 1330 Leyden, Suite 103 Denver, CO 80220
Connecticut	SIDS Information and Counseling Project Connecticut State Department of Health Services Maternal and Child Health Section 79 Elm Street Hartford, CT 06115	Carol Christoffers, R.N., M.S.W. Project Director (203) 566-7749 (Vacant) Project Coordinator (203) 566-7749
District of Columbia	SIDS Information and Counseling Project Department of Human Services Ambulatory Health Care Administration 1875 Connecticut Avenue, NW Eighth Floor Washington, D.C. 20009	Ishild Swoboda, M.D. Project Codirector (202) 673-6670 Carolyn French, R.N. Project Coordinator (202) 727-0395 702 Fifteenth Street, NE, Room 4 Washington, D.C. 20002

Florida	SIDS Information and Counseling Project Florida State Department of Health and Rehabilitative Services, Family Health Program 1317 Winewood Boulevard Tallahassee, FL 32301	J. Robert Griffin Project Codirector (904) 488-2834 Betty McEntire, Ph.D. Project Coordinator (904) 487-1502 Suite 261, Marathon Building Koger Executive Center 2574 Seagate Drive Tallahassee, FL 32301
Georgia	SIDS Information and Counseling Project Georgia Department of Human Resources Maternal and Child Health 47 Trinity Avenue Atlanta, GA 30334	Lillian P. Warnick, M.D. Project Director (404) 656-4830 Susan Williamson, R.N. Project Coordinator (404) 656-4830
Hawaii	Hawaii SIDS Information and Counseling Project Kapiolani Children's Medical Center 1319 Punahou Street Honolulu, HI 96826	Dexter S. Y. Seto, M.D. Project Director (808) 947-8567 Sharon Morton, R.N. Project Coordinator (808) 947-8567
Idaho	SIDS Information and Counseling Project Idaho Department of Health and Welfare Child Health Bureau Statehouse Boise, ID 83720	Zsolt Koppanyi, M.D. Project Director (208) 334-4136 Coleen Hughes, R.N., Ph.D. Project Coordinator (208) 334-4136
Illinois	SIDS Regional Center Loyola University Medical Center Building 54, Second Floor 2160 S. First Avenue Maywood, IL 60153	Julius Goldberg, Ph.D., Dr. P.H. Project Director (312) 531-3420 Milda Dargis, M.A. Project Coordinator (312) 531-3420

SIDS Information and
Counseling Project
Illinois Department of Public
Health
Division of Family Health
535 W. Jefferson Street
Springfield, IL 62761

Bernard J. Turnock,
M.D., M.P.H.
Project Director
(217) 782-2736

Lori Bennett
Project Coordinator
(217) 782-2736

Indiana

SIDS Information and
Counseling Project
Statewide SIDS Case
Management System
Indiana State Board of
Health
1330 W. Michigan Street
P.O. Box 1964
Indianapolis, IN 46206

Geraldine Wojtowicz,
R.N.
Project Director
(317) 633-8461

Dianna Oliver, R.N.
Project Coordinator
(317) 633-8461

Iowa

SIDS Information and
Counseling Project
Iowa State Department of
Health
Lucas State Office Building
Des Moines, IA 50319

John E. Goodrich, M.D.
Project Director
(515) 281-6646

Roger Chapman, M.S.W.
Project Coordinator
(515) 281-6646

Kentucky

SIDS Information and
Counseling Project
Kentucky Department for
Human Resources
Bureau for Health Services
Division for Maternal and
Child Health
275 E. Main Street
Frankfort, KY 40621

Patricia K. Nicol, M.D.
Project Director
(502) 564-3527

Ida Lyons, R.N.
Project Coordinator
(502) 564-3527

Maine

SIDS Information and
Counseling Project
Maine Department of
Human Services
Division of Public Health
Nursing
Statehouse
Augusta, ME 04333

Helen M. Zidowecki,
R.N., M.S.
Project Director
(207) 289-3259

Kathleen Jewett, R.N.,
M.S.
Project Coordinator
(207) 289-3259

Maryland	Maryland SIDS Information and Counseling Project University of Maryland School of Medicine Medical School Teaching Facility 10 S. Pine Street, Suite 400 Baltimore, MD 21201	Stanford B. Friedman, M.D. Project Director (301) 528-3542 Susan Woolsey, R.N., M.S. Assistant Director (301) 528-5062
Massachusetts	Massachusetts Center for SIDS Boston City Hospital Ambulatory Care Center, Fourth Floor South 818 Harrison Avenue Boston, MA 02118	Frederick Mandell, M.D. Project Codirector (617) 735-6000, Ext. 2876 Linda S. Goodale, R.N. Project Coordinator (617) 424-5741
Michigan	SIDS Information and Counseling Project Michigan Medical Legal Research and Education Association, Inc. 400 E. Lafayette Detroit, MI 48226	Werner Spitz, M.D. Project Director (313) 963-1528 Zoe Smialek, R.N. Project Coordinator (313) 963-1528
Minnesota	SIDS Information and Counseling Project Minnesota Children's Health Center 2525 Chicago Avenue S. Minneapolis, MN 55404	Ralph A. Franciosi, M.D. Project Codirector (612) 874-6285 Kathleen Fernbach, PHN Project Coordinator (612) 874-6285
Mississippi	SIDS Information and Counseling Project Mississippi State Board of Health Bureau of Personal Health Services P.O. Box 1700 Jackson, MS 39205	Terry Beck, M.S.W. Project Director (601) 354-6680 Judith Barber, A.C.S.W. Project Coordinator (601) 354-6680

Missouri	Missouri SIDS Information and Counseling Project St. Louis Regional Maternal and Child Health Council 5600 Oakland, Room G-350A St. Louis, MO 63110	Laura Hillman, M.D. Project Codirector (314) 454-2141 Sharon Hollander, M.S.W. Project Coordinator (314) 644-4100
Nebraska	SIDS Information and Counseling Project Nebraska Department of Health Division of Maternal and Child Health 301 Centennial Mall S. P.O. Box 95007 Lincoln, NB 68509	Robert S. Grant, M.D., M.P.H. Project Director (402) 471-2907 Jane Jensen, R.N. Project Coordinator (402) 344-3960 VNA of Omaha 4500 Ames Avenue Omaha, NB 68104
New Hampshire	SIDS Information and Counseling Project New Hampshire Department of Health and Welfare Division of Public Health Services Bureau of Public Health Nursing Health and Welfare Building Hazen Drive Concord, NH 03301	Elizabeth A. Burtt, R.N., M.P.H. Project Director (603) 271-4493 Carole T. Young-Kleinfeld, M.S.W. Project Coordinator (603) 271-4524
New Jersey	SIDS Information and Counseling Project New Jersey State Department of Health Maternal and Child Health Program John Fitch Plaza, Box 1540 Trenton, NJ 08625	Margaret Gregory, M.D. Project Director (609) 292-5616 Elizabeth Broderick, R.N., M.S.N. Project Coordinator (609) 292-5616
New Mexico	SIDS Information and Counseling Project University of New Mexico School of Medicine	James T. Weston, M.D. Project Director (505) 277-3053

Office of the Medical
Investigator and New
Mexico Center for
Forensic and
Environmental Science
Albuquerque, NM 87131

Beverly White, R.N.
Project Coordinator
(505) 277-3053

New York

New York City Information
and Counseling Project
Office of Medical Examiner
520 First Avenue, Room 506
New York, NY 10016

Jean Pakter, M.D.
Project Codirector
(212) 566-7076

Christine Blenninger,
R.N.
Project Coordinator
(212) 686-8854

Genessee Region SIDS
Information and
Counseling Project
University of Rochester
Medical Center
601 Elmwood Avenue, P.O.
Box 777
Rochester, NY 14642

Margaret T. Colgan,
M.D.
Project Codirector
(716) 275-7758

Gabrielle Weiss, R.N.
Project Coordinator
(716) 275-7758

SIDS Information and
Counseling Project
Sudden Infant Death
Syndrome Regional Center
School of Social Welfare
Health Sciences Center
State University of New
York
Stony Brook, NY 11794

Dean Ruth A. Brandwein,
Ph.D.
Project Director
(516) 246-2582

Jean Elizabeth Scully,
M.S.W.
Project Coordinator
(516) 246-2582

North Carolina

North Carolina SIDS
Information and
Counseling Project
Department of Human
Resources
Division of Health Services
Maternal and Child Health
Branch
P.O. Box 2091
Raleigh, NC 27602

Jimmie L. Rhyne, M.D.
Project Director
(919) 733-7791

Kay McNeill, R.N.,
M.P.H.
Project Coordinator
(919) 733-7791

Ohio	Ohio SIDS Information and Counseling Project Ohio Department of Health Bureau of Maternal and Child Health 246 N. High Street, P.O. Box 118 Columbus, OH 43216	Marsha Herring, R.N. Project Director (614) 466-8804
Oklahoma	SIDS Information and Counseling Project Oklahoma State Department of Health 1000 NE 10th Street P.O. Box 53551 Oklahoma City, OK 73152	Edd D. Rhoades, M.D. Project Director (405) 271-4471 Wallace Johnson, M.S.W. Project Coordinator (405) 271-4471
Oregon	Oregon SIDS Information and Counseling Project Portland State University College of Social Science P.O. Box 751 Portland, OR 97207	Dean George C. Hoffman, Ph.D. Project Director (503) 229-3911 Janice Cram, B.A. Project Coordinator (503) 229-3962
Pennsylvania	Pennsylvania SIDS Information and Counseling Project Pennsylvania SIDS Resource Center One Children's Center Philadelphia, PA 19104	George Peckham, M.D. Project Director (215) 472-2229 Michael D'Antonio, Ph.D. Project Coordinator (215) 472-2229
Rhode Island	SIDS Information and Counseling Project Rhode Island Department of Health Division of Family Health Cannon Building 75 Davis Street, Room 302 Providence, RI 02908	William H. Hollinshead III, M.D. Project Director (401) 277-2231 (Vacant) Project Coordinator (401) 277-2231

South Carolina	SIDS Information and Counseling Project South Carolina Department of Health & Environmental Control Bureau of Maternal and Child Care 2600 Bull Street Columbia, SC 29201	Dorothy Bon, M.S.W. Project Director (803) 758-8553 Anna Weir, S.W. Project Coordinator (803) 758-8553
South Dakota	SIDS Information and Counseling Project South Dakota Department of Health Division of Health Services Joe Foss Building Pierre, SD 57501	Allen Krom, M.S.W. Project Director (605) 773-3737 Project Coordinator
Tennessee	SIDS Information and Counseling Project Metropolitan Government of Nashville and Davidson County 311 Twenty-third Avenue N. Nashville, TN 37203	J. M. Bistowish, M.D. Project Director (615) 327-9313 Anita Davis, R.N. Project Coordinator (615) 327-9313
Texas	SIDS Information and Counseling Project University of Texas Health Science Center at Dallas Department of Pediatrics 5323 Harry Hines Boulevard Dallas, TX 75235	Arthur G. Weinberg, M.D. Project Director (214) 637-3820 Leslie U. Malone, M.A. Project Coordinator (214) 688-2796
	SIDS Information and Counseling Project Harris County Health Department 2370 Rice Boulevard Box 25249 Houston, TX 77005	Francine Jensen, M.D. Project Director (713) 526-1841 Elvia Rios, R.N. Project Coordinator (512) 458-7700 Division of Maternal and Child Health Texas Department of Health 1100 W. 49th Street Austin, TX 78756

Bexar County SIDS
Information and
Counseling Project
The University of Texas
Health Science Center at
San Antonio Medical
School
Department of Pediatrics
7703 Floyd Curl Drive
San Antonio, TX 78284

Valerie Ostrower, M.D.
Project Director
(512) 223-6361, Ext. 295

Patty Villareal, R.N.
Project Coordinator
(512) 691-6481
Bexar County SIDS
Project
Robert B. Green Hospital
Room 111E
4502 Medical Drive
San Antonio, TX 78284

Utah

SIDS Information and
Counseling Project
Utah Department of Health
Division of Family Health
Services
Bureau of Maternal and
Child Health
44 Medical Drive
Salt Lake City, UT 84113

Thomas L. Wells, M.D.
Project Director
(801) 533-4084

Echomae Anderson, R.N.
Project Coordinator
(801) 533-6161

Vermont

Vermont SIDS Information
and Counseling Project
Vermont Department of
Health
115 Colchester Avenue
Burlington, VT 05401

Roberta Coffin, M.D.
Project Director
(802) 862-5701

Claire Lefrancois, R.N.,
M.P.H.
Project Coordinator
(802) 862-5701

Washington

SIDS Northwest Regional
Center
Children's Orthopedic
Hospital & Medical Center
4800 Sand Point Way NE
Seattle, WA 98105

Nora E. Davis, M.D.
Project Director
(206) 634-5323

Susan Dolan, R.N.
Project Coordinator
(206) 634-5323

West Virginia

Statewide SIDS Information
and Counseling Project
West Virginia University
Department of Pediatrics/
Medical Center
Morgantown, WV 26506

David Myerberg, M.D.
Project Director
(304) 293-4451

Barbara Judy, M.S.W.
Project Coordinator
(304) 293-4451

Wisconsin

SIDS Information and
  Counseling Project
Wisconsin Dept. of Health
  and Social Services
Division of Health
P.O. Box 309
Madison, WI 53701

Ruth Robinson, M.S.W.
Project Director
(608) 266-2661

Connie Guist, R.N.
Project Coordinator
(414) 931-4049
Wisconsin SIDS Center
Milwaukee Children's
  Hospital
1700 W. Wisconsin
  Avenue
Milwaukee, WI 53233

PROFESSIONAL GROUPS

AMERICAN ASSOCIATION FOR MARRIAGE AND FAMILY THERAPY
AAMFT SUBDIVISIONS (PRESIDENT OR CONTACT PERSON)

ALABAMA
Mary Anne Armour, M.A.
118 N. Ross Street
Auburn, AL 36830
(205) 887-9764

ARIZONA
James Hine, M. Div.
4961 N. Calle Luisa
Tucson, AZ 85718
(602) 299-6007

CALIFORNIA (Northern)
Bernice Itkin, M.A.
435 Euclid Avenue
San Francisco, CA 94118
(415) 387-0486

CALIFORNIA (Southern)
Chas. and Susan Hansen
3821 Fourth Avenue
San Diego, CA 92103
(714) 293-3381

COLORADO
Richard Passoth, M.Ed.
926 S. Corona
Denver, CO 80209
(303) 355-1503

CONNECTICUT
Gerald Arndt, Ed.D.
56 Woodhaven Drive
Trumbull, CT 06611
(203) 336-3631

FLORIDA
Ann Ruben, Ph.D.
16499 NE Nineteenth Avenue
North Miami Beach, FL 33162
(305) 949-7536

GEORGIA
William Neville, Ed.D.
2959 Piedmont
Atlanta, GA 30305
(404) 231-1414

HAWAII
Margery Terpstra, Ph.D.
1750 Kalakaua, #2110
Honolulu, HI 96826
(808) 946-9128

ILLINOIS
E. J. Lyons, M.S.W.
326 Waverly Street
Park Forest, IL 60466
(312) 748-3250

INDIANA
Juanita Leonard, M.A.
2815 E. 62nd St.
Indianapolis, IN 46220
(317) 257-1491

IOWA
Charles Cole, Ph.D.
RR 4
Ames, IA 50010
(515) 232-2524

KANSAS
Anthony Jurich, Ph.D.
Kansas State University
Dept. of Family and Child
Manhattan, KS 66506
(913) 532-5510

KENTUCKY
E. Celeste Gorman, M.A.
5135 Dixie Highway, #23
Louisville, KY 40216
(502) 447-4005

LOUISIANA
Lamar Wilkinson, Ed.D.
162 India
Shreveport, LA 71115
(318) 797-6980

MAINE
James M. Moran, M.S.
RR 3, 10 Collinwood Park
South Windham, ME 04082
(207) 892-9765

MASSACHUSETTS
Samuel Pizzi, M.Ed.
220 Linden Street
Holyoke, MA 01040
(413) 538-9070

MICHIGAN
J. Herbert Mueller, M.S.W.
406 N. Revena
Ann Arbor, MI 48103
(313) 995-2736

MISSISSIPPI
Joanne Stevens, Ed.D.
University of Southern Mississippi
Box 8265
Hattiesburg, MS 39401
(601) 266-7111

MISSOURI
James McKenna, M.S.W.
522 N. New Ballas Road, #136
St. Louis, MO 63141
(314) 432-4522

NEBRASKA
Richard Murdoch, Ph.D.
1517 S. 114th Street
Omaha, NB 68144
(402) 333-7466

NEVADA
William Denney, M.A.
1325 Airmotive Way, #250
Reno, NV 89502
(702) 826-7722

NEW HAMPSHIRE
Kenneth A. Fiery, D.Min.
2 Wellman Avenue
Nashua, NH 03060
(603) 883-7904

NEW JERSEY
Richard Bundy, Th.M.
24 N. Third Avenue, #20
Highland Park, NJ 08904
(201) 828-7447

NEW MEXICO
Carroll Whiteside, Ph.D.
901 Bel Aire
Rosewell, NM 88201
(505) 624-0350

NEW YORK
Ruth Neubauer, Ed.D.
21 Rushby Way
Yonkers, NY 10701
(914) 476-9717

NORTH CAROLINA
Edward Mel Markowski, Ph.D.
801 E. First Street
Greenville, NC 27834
(919) 752-0072

OHIO
Paul Crabtree, Ph.D.
Shawnee State College
940 2nd Street
Portsmouth, OH 45662
(614) 354-3205

OKLAHOMA
Timothy Welch, M.S.W.
6262 S. Sheridan
Tulsa, OK 74133
(918) 492-8200

OREGON
Bill Kennemer, Ph.D.
Lake Plaza
6901 SE Lake Road
Milwaukie, OR 97222
(503) 654-3635

PENNSYLVANIA
Richard McCune, D.Min.
1135 E. Chocolate Avenue, #201
Hershey, PA 17033
(717) 534-2134

SOUTH CAROLINA
H. B. Free, M.S.S.W.
Family Service
30 Lockwood Boulevard
Charleston, SC 29401
(803) 723-4566

TENNESSEE
Myrtle Qualls, M.A.
Route 1, Box 328
Hendersonville, TN 37075
(615) 824-8016

TEXAS
Robert E. Buxbaum, D.Min.
4245 Centerview Drive, #140
San Antonio, TX 78228
(512) 734-6117

UTAH
Veon Smith, Jr., D.S.W.
9528 Caledonia Circle
South Jordan, UT 84065
(801) 968-6410

VERMONT
Charles Campbell, D.Min.
81 Summer
Springfield, VT 05156
(802) 885-4254

VIRGINIA
Michael Sporakowski, Ph.D.
702 Patrick Henry
Blacksburg, VA 24060
(703) 961-5434

WASHINGTON
Douglas Anderson, Ph.D.
29933 Third Avenue SW
Federal Way, WA 98003
(206) 839-0344

WISCONSIN
James Gebhard, M.S.W.
Box 428
Stevens Point, WI 54481
(715) 344-2500

WYOMING
Ray Muh, Ph.D.
Box 1005
2322 Evans Avenue
Cheyenne, WY 82001
(307) 634-9653

NATIONAL MENTAL HEALTH ASSOCIATIONS

Note: The following listing does not constitute an endorsement but is provided only as another possible avenue of help. A number of these divisions and chapters conduct educational programs concerning grief and bereavement, and all their affiliates serve as referral agencies. It will be necessary to check if the particular chapter near you has an existing program or assistance available to bereaved parents. You may also wish to look under "Grief Centers."

Mental Health Association in
Alabama
306 Whitman Street
Montgomery, AL 36104

Alaska Mental Health Association
5401 Cordova Street, #304
Anchorage, AK 99503

Mental Health Association in
Arizona
1515 E. Osborn Road
Phoenix, AZ 85014

Mental Health Association in
Arkansas
3006 Meyer Building
Hot Springs, AR 71901

Mental Health Association in
California
1211 "H" Street, Suite F
Sacramento, CA 95814

Mental Health Association in
Colorado
252 Clayton Street, Garden #2
Denver, CO 80206

Mental Health Association in
Connecticut
56 Arbor Street
Hartford, CT 06106

Mental Health Association in
Delaware
1813 N. Franklin Street
Wilmington, DE 19802

D.C. Mental Health Association
2101 16th Street NW
Washington, D.C. 20009

Mental Health Association of
Florida
Suite 207, Myrick Building
132 E. Colonial Drive
Orlando, FL 32801

Mental Health Association in
  Georgia
100 Edgewood Avenue NE, #502
Atlanta, GA 30303

Mental Health Association in
  Hawaii
200 N. Vineyard Boulevard, #507
Honolulu, HI 96817

Mental Health Association in
  Idaho
3105½ State Street
Boise, ID 83703

Mental Health Association in
  Illinois
1418 S. 7th Street
Springfield, IL 62703

Mental Health Association in
  Indiana
1433 N. Meridian Street
Indianapolis, IN 46202

Mental Health Association of Iowa
315 E. 5th Street
Des Moines, IA 50315

Mental Health Association in
  Kansas
1205 Harrison Street
Topeka, KS 66612

Kentucky Association for Mental
  Health
310 W. Liberty Street, #106
Louisville, KY 40202

Mental Health Association in
  Louisiana
1528 Jackson Avenue
New Orleans, LA 70130

Mental Health Association of
  Maryland
325 E. 25th Street
Baltimore, MD 21218

Massachusetts Association for
  Mental Health
1 Walnut Street
Boston, MA 02108

Mental Health Association in
  Michigan
15920 W. Twelve Mile Road
Southfield, MI 48076

Mental Health Association in
  Minnesota
6715 Minnetonka Boulevard,
  #209–10
St. Louis Park, MN 55426

Mental Health Association in
  Mississippi
P.O. Box 5041
Jackson, MS 39216

Mental Health Association in
  Missouri
P.O. Box 1667
Jefferson City, MO 65102

Mental Health Association in
  Montana
201 S. Last Chance Gulch, #207
Helena, MT 59601

New Hampshire Association for
  Mental Health
11 South Main
Concord, NH 03301

Mental Health Association in New
  Jersey
60 S. Fullerton Avenue
Montclair, NJ 07042

Mental Health Association in
  North Carolina
3701 National Drive, #222
Raleigh, NC 27612

Mental Health Association in
  North Dakota
P.O. Box 160
Bismarck, ND 58501

Mental Health Association in Ohio
50 W. Broad Street, #2440
Columbus, OH 43215

Mental Health Association in
Oklahoma
1140 North West 32
Oklahoma City, OK 73118

Mental Health Association in
Oregon
718 W. Burnside, Room 301
Portland, OR 97209

Mental Health Association in
Pennsylvania
1207 Chestnut Street
Philadelphia, PA 19107

Mental Health Association in
Rhode Island
57 Hope Street
Providence, RI 02906

South Dakota Mental Health
Association
101½ S. Pierre Street, Box 353
Pierre, SD 57501

Tennessee Mental Health
Association
250 Venture Circle
Nashville, TN 37228

Texas Association for Mental
Health
4600 Burnet Road
Austin, TX 78756

Utah Association for Mental
Health
982 E. 3300 South
Salt Lake City, UT 84106

Mental Health Association in
Virginia
1806 Chantilly Street, #203
Richmond, VA 23230

Mental Health Association in
Washington
500 John Street
Seattle, WA 98109

West Virginia Association for
Mental Health
702½ Lee Street
Charleston, WV 25301

Wisconsin Association for Mental
Health
119 E. Mifflin, Box 1486
Madison, WI 53701

ELEGY FOR PHILIPPE-MAGUILEN
October 17, 1958–June 7, 1981

By Léopold-Sédar Senghor
Former President of Sénégal

To Colette, his mother

I

The days have passed in gloomy *boubous** and the
    nights-days without sleep.
The mourners have exhausted the depth of their tears
    without soothing our obstinate sadness.
Against it, we searched the foundations of the old
    residence
Where our hope was resting, and the park guards the steps,
    the play, the joy of generations.
When we turn the corner of the moss-grown wall, there
Once again are the tenderly mixed perfumes of honeysuckle
    and of jasmine.
At six in the evening, over the turf which was being
    grazed by the swallows with their little sharp cries
It was already transparent, the September light, as on
    Gorée Island
After a winter rain. And we saw the Angels fly on their
    translucent wings.
You remember, as it embalmed happiness, the infant
    flower of change?
Listen, therefore, to its voice vibrant like the
    trombone, singing
    Steal away to Jesus
Then the telephone rang like the sound of a gun
    in my heart?

*African dress

II

It was the seventh of June, it was Whit-Sunday.
You were all haloed in white and rose, my
    *Normande,** under your aerial hooded cape
To receive the splendor of mystery.
In the clear light, your eyes, nostalgic, sang the
    "Absent," when
Suddenly the ring of the white telephone, which
    always caused you to tremble with pale shudders
The flash of lightening. And evaporating flower, suddenly,
    you fell in my arms,
And creepers, we clasp the infant of love, absent
    and beautiful like Zous, the Ethiopian.
It is his call, the ring of the long telephone, and
There we are in the great white Bird, like a bright arrow
and the oblique wings. And there it goes piercing the
    wall at the speed of sound
And from there at twice the speed of sound, straight over
    Cape Verde, a dark silhouette, on the blue ocean.
It is the great white God that defies space, but does
    not know that I did not say give
I said keep the life of an infant: the white tears
    of his mother.
There, then, is our infant, the mixed breath of our nostrils,
    fading out, Ha!
In its smell of laurel and rose, even as five women,
    yes, five *Normandes,* gathered groomed and
    knitted
To make him the son of happiness.

III

And I said "No!" to the doctor. "My son is not dead
    it is impossible"

*From Normandy (his wife)

Pardon me, Lord, and sweep away my blasphemy, but
    it is impossible.
No, no! Those who are coddled by the gods do not
    die so young.
No! You are not a jealous God like Baal who
    fed on *éphèbes.*
Of our waning autumn, he was the spring;
    his smile was of the dawn.
His eyes profound, a crystal-clear sky and full of humor.
He was life and the cause of living for this mother, a
    lamp keeping vigil over night and life.
Brutally you snatched him from us, like a treasure by
    the greatest highway robber
Who has said to us: "The road is tired, the *marigot**
    is tired, the sky
Is tired." We had given everything to this country, to
    this continent of ours:
The days and the nights and the vigils, the fatigue, the
    pain and the fighting among the assembled nations.
Now a Senegalese over Senegalese has been made the
    Normande
    of long lineage, with her eyes of green and golden *moire*
And her son she made the son of Senegalese soil, and
    one day, he would repose
Deep in the ground of Mamanguedj, † near Diogoye—le lion.‡
But you already claimed him, the son of love, in order to
    redeem our unsubdued people.
As if three hundred years of toil had not been enough,
    O terrible God of Abraham!
And you have crucified his mother, high on a tree of
    cinders and of ice.
And the mother's faith has staggered under the lightening

*Pond
†River
‡His grand-father

and thunder, like the shattered cedar that shades
the vast house.
She has been elevated, but we are elevated, having faith
at heart.
It is Paul in the dust, and on the road to Damascus, all
of a sudden, the lights.
Lord, it is impenetrable, the labyrinth of your designs:
one loses its thread when not devoured by
the *Minotaure*.
So thy will be done
Let our son, on the day of the resurrection, be raised
like the sun of the dawn
In the transfiguration of his beauty!

IV

He was washed for the heavenly wedding, perfumed with
fresh Vetiver
His long body was laid down in a precious wooden coffin.
Young men, his comrades lifted him up, carried him high
on their shoulders
Under the spring flowers, the songs that were like palms,
his people providing a procession for him
All his people were gathered together like braided wreaths.
Priests and Marabouts,* employees and workers, delegations
of friendly nations
The notables surely; I said here is Senegal rising
from its depth!
Peasants, Fishermen, shepherds, and all the youth were
pressed together without a seam
From Bakel to Bandafassy, from Ndialakhar and Ndiongalor†
to the red Cape.
And all along the streets in tears, from the black avenues
prostrated under the June sun

*Muslim priest
†Counties in Senegal

The reverent youth, carrying him in their hearts, like a
    green gold medal.
But they know, these so diligent students, that only live
    the dead whose name is chanted
And here they are competing with the virgins of Ndayane* on
    a spotless loin cloth
Chanting gymnic songs, as previously on resounding theaters.
Here is Guignane and Guilena, Soukeina, Rokhaya
    Dominique
    Doris, and Linda and Melinda
Who sing: *"Dior de Joal!*
"Burst with applause when the champion of
    Gnilane-Le-Doucet† enters.
"This is the horseman with the black helmet, plumed
    with purple
"Who tames thoroughbred horses over quick sands.
"He is elegant to the antagonist, attracting attention like
    flowers to a young girl.
"A twig clamped from Viking on Tabor, a horseman on
    the veiled plank
"There he is a bronze bust launched, and a floating head band
"Whose message is written in green and gold, in graceful
    lines on the sea of wonders,
"O Prince of Grace, we are always thirsty for your smile."

V

You, who have loved profoundly, will be profoundly forgiven:
You tenderly loved your father and your mother, your
    brothers
and all like brothers, the landlord, the blind using their
    hands as antenna, the rheumy-eyed beggars
The Black and the *Toubab*‡ all white, men of the rising sun

*River
†His grandmother
‡African term for a white man

The Arab and the Berber, the Moor, my little Moor
My Bengali, as we used to call you, the Tutsi and the Hutu.
When comes the day of love, of your heavenly wedding
The cherubs will receive you on their blue silky wings,
    they will lead you
To the right of resurrected Christ, the tender Lamb of light,
    for which you had been yearning
And among the black Serophins, will sing the martyrs
    of Uganda.
And you will accompany them to the organ, as you did at
    Verson,
Dressed in white white linen, washed in the blood of
    the Lamb, your own blood.
Plunging down your fine nervous hand, you will establish
    basses and contraltos in the polyphony.
Thus you will advance smoothly, like a frieze of slender
    lingueres, * the choir of the Powers.
They will evolve slowly slowly, weaving noble delicate figures
Until a sudden movement from the abyss, and
You will underline the faintness of a cry of pain, of joy,
Even a cry of paradise, which is happiness.

*Queen, mother

SUGGESTED READING

ADULTS

Agee, James A. *A Death in the Family.* New York: Obolinsky McDowell, 1957.

Anthony, S. *The Child's Discovery of Death.* New York: Harcourt, Brace & Co., 1940.

Borg, Susan, and Judith Lasker. *When Pregnancy Fails: Families Coping with Miscarriage, Stillbirth, and Infant Death.* Boston: Beacon Press, 1981.

Davidson, Dr. Glen. *Living with Dying.* Minneapolis: Augsburg Publishing House, 1975.

Dempsey, David. *The Way We Die.* New York: Macmillan Publishing Co., Inc., 1975.

Fiefel, H. (ed.). *The Meaning of Death.* New York: McGraw-Hill Book Co., 1959.

Gordon, David C. *Overcoming the Fear of Death.* Baltimore: Penguin Books, Inc., 1970.

Grollman, Earl A. *Concerning Death: A Practical Guide for the Living.* Boston: Beacon Press, 1974.

———. *Talking About Death: A Dialogue Between Parent and Child.* Boston: Beacon Press, 1976.

——— (ed.). *Explaining Death to Children.* Boston: Beacon Press, 1967.

Gunther, John. *Death Be Not Proud.* New York: Harper & Row, 1971.

Hendin, D. *Death As a Fact of Life.* New York: Warner Paperbacks, 1974.

Irish, Jerry A. *A Boy Thirteen.* Philadelphia, Westminster Press, 1975.

Jackson, Edgar. *Telling a Child About Death.* New York: Channel Press, 1965.

Kastenbaum, Robert, and Ruth Aisenberg. *The Psychology of Death.* New York: Springer Publishing Co., Inc., 1972.

Kübler-Ross, Elisabeth. *Death: The Final Stage of Growth.* Englewood Cliffs, N.J.: Prentice-Hall, Inc., 1975.

———. *Living with Death and Dying.* New York: Macmillan Publishing Co., Inc., 1981.

Langone, John. *Death Is a Noun*. Boston & Toronto: Little, Brown and Company, 1972.

Lefebvre, Leo C., Jr. *Sudden Infant Death Syndrome: Its Impact on Parents, Grandparents, Neighbors and Friends—From a Father's Perspective*. Revised April 1979. Published by The Council of Guilds for Infant Survival, Inc., Washington, D.C.

Lepp, Ignace. *Death and Its Mysteries*. New York: Macmillan Publishing Co., Inc., 1968.

Lifton, Robert J., and Eric Olson. *Living and Dying*. New York: Praeger, 1974.

Lund, D. *Eric*. Philadelphia: J. B. Lippincott Co., 1974.

Miles, Margaret S. *The Grief of Parents When a Child Dies*. Oak Brook, Ill., The Compassionate Friends, 1980.

Moody, Raymond A., Jr. *Life After Life*. New York: Bantam Books, Inc., 1976.

Peppers, Larry, and Ronald Knapp. *Motherhood and Mourning*. New York: Praeger, 1980.

Raab, Robert A. *Coping with Death*. New York: Richards Rosen Press, Inc., 1978.

Ring, Kenneth. *Life at Death*. New York: Coward, McCann & Geoghegan, 1980.

Rubin, T. *The Angry Book*. New York: Macmillan Publishing Co., Inc., 1969.

Rudolph, Marguerita. *Should the Children Know?: Encounters with Death in the Lives of Children*. New York: Schocken Books, 1978.

Schiff, Harriet Sarnoff. *The Bereaved Parent*. New York: Crown Publishers, Inc., 1977.

Schulz, Richard. *The Psychology of Death, Dying and Bereavement*. Reading, Mass.: Addison-Wesley Publishing Company, 1978.

Sherman, Harold. *The Dead Are Alive*. Harold Sherman, Publisher, 1981. Mountain View, Arkansas 75260.

Simos, Bertha G. *A Time to Grieve*. New York: Irvington Publishers, Inc., 1980.

Smart, Vivian. *The Long Search*. Boston: Little, Brown and Company, 1977.

Stein, Sara Bonnet. *About Dying*. New York: Walker & Co., 1974.

Temes, Robert. *Living with an Empty Chair—A Guide Through Grief*. New York: Irvington Publishers, 1977.

Toynbee, Arnold. *Man's Concern with Death*. New York: McGraw-Hill Book Company, 1968.

Weir, Robert F. (ed.). *Death in Literature*. New York: Columbia University Press, 1980.

Wolf, A. *Helping Your Child Understand Death.* New York: Child Study Association of America, 1958.

CHILDREN

Alcott, L. M. *Little Women.* New York: Grosset & Dunlap, 1947.

Bernstein, Joanne E. *When People Die.* New York: Dutton, 1977.

Brown, M. W. *The Dead Bird.* New York: Young Scott Books, 1958.

Carner, Charles. *Tawny.* New York: Macmillan Publishing Co., Inc., 1978.

Coburn, J. B. *Anne and the Sand Dobbies.* New York: Seabury Press, 1964.

Graeber, Charlotte. *Mustard.* New York: Macmillan Publishing Co., Inc., 1982.

Greene, Constance. *Beat the Turtle Drum.* New York: Viking Press, 1976.

Kennedy, Richard. *Come Again in the Spring.* New York: Harper & Row, 1976.

Lee, V. *The Magic Moth.* New York: Seabury Press, 1972.

LeShan, Eda. *Learning to Say Good-Bye.* New York: Macmillan Publishing Co., Inc., 1976.

McHugh, Mary. *Young People Talk About Death.* New York and London: Franklin Watts, 1980.

Miles, M. *Annie and the Old One.* Boston: Little, Brown and Company, 1971.

Roch, A. *The Thanksgiving Treasure.* New York: Alfred A. Knopf, 1972.

Rudolph, Marguerita. *Should the Children Know?: Encounters with Death in the Lives of Children.* New York: Schocken Books, 1978.

Smith, D. G. *A Taste of Blackberries.* New York: Crowell Co., 1973.

Viorst, Judith. *The Tenth Good Thing About Barney.* New York: Atheneum, 1971.

White, E. B. *Charlotte's Web.* New York: Harper & Row, 1952.

INDEX